Irene Thompson is a journalist and teacher of English as a foreign language. She has been environment columnist for the Press Association, US-based education writer for the *Daily Mail*, editor of the *Coalport Collector* magazine and co-founder and editor with journalist husband, John Bell, of a newspaper for British tourists in South Florida.

GW00359613

# NARROW
# ESCAPES
## AND
# LUCKY
# BREAKS

Published by John Blake Publishing Ltd,
3 Bramber Court, 2 Bramber Road,
London W14 9PB, England

www.blake.co.uk

First published in paperback in 2007

ISBN: 978-1-84454-443-1

British Library Cataloguing-in-Publication Data:

A catalogue record for this book is available from the British Library.

Design by www.envydesign.co.uk

Printed in Great Britain by Mackays of Chatham Ltd, Chatham, Kent

1 3 5 7 9 10 8 6 4 2

© Text copyright Irene Thompson, 2007
Cartoons © Mike Mosedale
www.londoncartoonists.co.uk

Papers used by John Blake Publishing are natural, recyclable products made
from wood grown in sustainable forests. The manufacturing processes conform
to the environmental regulations of the country of origin.

# NARROW ESCAPES AND LUCKY BREAKS

### THE WORLD'S MOST AMAZING TRUE STORIES OF CHEATING DEATH AND SURVIVING AGAINST THE ODDS.

## IRENE THOMPSON

JOHN BLAKE

# ACKNOWLEDGEMENTS

No book can be written without assistance from others, whether that help is in the form of information or moral support. In the former, I am particularly indebted to the authors of well-documented books on the more remarkable miracles that have occurred at Lourdes, including *I Accept These Facts* by Michel Agnellet and *Modern Miraculous Cures* by Dr Francois Leuret, former President of the Medical Bureau and Bureau of Scientific Studies of Lourdes. The research and conclusions of these eminent physicians provide weighty evidence to support the claims of those who went to the shrine in desperate health and

came away cured. D Scott Rogo's book *Miracles.
A Scientific Exploration of Wondrous Phenomena* was
also a useful source of reference in this area.

I have been able to utilise the wide resources of
internet library services to locate miracle
accounts from all parts of the world. This has
sometimes involved ferreting through hundreds
of articles to find a snippet of information or a
name I could follow up in other ways – much
like unravelling a ball of string. Finding a good
miracle at the end of the search was always
rewarding.

My local librarians have plumbed the depths of
their archives and dusted off ancient tomes, or
combed the counties to round up books in order
to meet my research needs.

I would also like to thank William A Burt,
author of *Blessed by Miracles*, for sharing his
extensive knowledge with me.

Finally, I would like to thank those who
delighted in the concept of this book and had
faith in its completion. Their enthusiasm and
encouragement were invaluable during the
solitary occupation of research and writing.

# CONTENTS

# CHAPTER ONE:
# Escape and Survival

# ESCAPE AND SURVIVAL

A Hollywood producer couldn't have dreamed up a disaster movie like it. The plane was packed with holidaymakers bound for Malaga from Birmingham. Suddenly, at 17,000 feet, the windscreen blew and the captain, Tim Lancaster, was sucked out. Quick-thinking steward Nigel Ogden saved his life by grabbing Tim's legs as the aircraft plummeted out of control at nearly 400 mph through some of the most congested skies in the world.

Tim's shirt had been pulled off his back and his body was bent upwards, doubled over the top of the plane. Everything in the cockpit was rapidly being sucked out and another steward gripped on to Nigel's trouser belt to stop him going, too. They were spiralling at 80 feet a second with no autopilot and no radio. Nigel could feel his arms freezing and being pulled from their sockets as he struggled to hold on to Tim's body.

Crew members managed to unwrap Tim's legs from the controls, enabling the co-pilot to take over. Then Tim slipped in Nigel's grasp until his body was wrapped around the windows with his bloody face banging against the glass, his arms flailing, his eyes fixed wide in terror. It was a horrific sight that Nigel will relive forever. He was sure the captain was dead.

But, after an amazingly smooth landing, all the passengers walked off the aircraft unscathed. Even more incredibly, Tim survived with only frostbite and arm fractures. Nigel returned to flying only briefly, before retiring early on the grounds of ill health.

Why isn't Genelle Guzman-McMillan dead? The last 9/11 survivor to be pulled from the wreckage of the Twin Towers doesn't know the answer. All she knows is that while 2,819 people perished around her, she was miraculously spared when her building collapsed and she was trapped beneath a heap of concrete rubble for more than 26 hours.

A clerical worker on the 64th floor of the North Tower, Genelle, then 30, and her colleagues began the long descent to safety after the first terrorist plane hit the building. They managed to reach the 13th floor when there was an almighty crash and the walls collapsed around them. Genelle's body tumbled into the abyss but somehow stopped falling when it hit an air pocket.

Her head was pinned between two pieces of concrete, her legs trapped in the wreckage of the stairway and her right hand caught under one leg. Only her left hand was free. It was eerily silent and dark, but she was alive. She felt around her for other survivors, but there was nobody. Then her hand brushed against a lifeless body lying next to her. She recoiled in horror, but later discovered that it was a

5

fireman and that the reflective bands on his uniform had saved her life; they were picked up in the beam of her rescuers' torches in the vast black acres of destruction.

Genelle escaped with a crushed right leg and minor injuries, but has since confounded doctors who said she'd need a leg brace for life. While her physical scars have healed, the nightmares continue.

Eight-year-old Justin Stiner was proud of the fact that he didn't cry when he fell from a roof on to a steel post, which impaled him through the heart. His mum, Amanda, marvels at the miracle that saved his life after the freak accident in Sierra Vista, Arizona, USA.

Justin was playing in his back garden with his sister and a group of children when he decided to climb a tree and scramble onto a neighbour's roof. The children watched in horror as Justin slipped and plunged 12 feet onto the stake, which was being used for coiling a garden hose. He dangled face down from where he was pinioned until the emergency services arrived and tried to decide what they should do. If they pulled him off the rod, he would bleed to death. If they cut it, the vibration and movement could kill him. Their only option was to hold the boy perfectly still and gently saw through the stake to cut him free.

'He never whimpered,' said fire captain Bob Miller. 'This kid was truly a little hero.'

Justin was flown to a trauma unit where, during emergency surgery, doctors found the half-inch rod had pierced his heart and severed his jugular vein. But it had missed two major arteries by a fraction of an inch. Hitting these would definitely have killed him. Justin was out of intensive care within 48 hours and sitting up in bed playing computer games.

'How many people get this kind of injury and survive?' said Dr Phillip Richemont. 'It's a one-in-a-billion miracle!'

To escape from the jaws of death once may be considered good fortune. But Randall

Champion reckons that to escape twice from the same killer definitely qualifies as miraculous.

The Florida electricity-company repairman was knocked unconscious when he accidentally brushed against a 4,200-volt power line. He was left dangling precariously from the top of a telegraph pole by his safety belt until a colleague rescued him.

Several years later, Randall was in a lift bucket at the top of a pole when he touched a cable which shot a massive 26,000 volts through his body – the same amount given on Death Row's electric chair. He was rushed to hospital with severe body burns and doctors feared that his heart or lungs would give out from the severe shock. But Randall survived again.

A family beach outing turned into a scene from a horror film when teacher Janice Poupard was struck by a huge bolt of lightning.

One moment Janet, 37, was heading back to the car with her husband and two children,

8

ahead of an impending storm. Then Janet's body was engulfed in flames and her skin began turning black from burns. Shocked onlookers screamed as they saw smoke billowing from her body and hair.

The bolt had entered her back beneath her right shoulder like a gunshot wound and it was so powerful that it melted her gold necklace and turned the metal underwiring in her bra red hot. Janet was unconscious for eight hours and it was a month before she could walk. Skin grafts have left scars beneath her breasts and on her thighs.

'But it's a miracle she survived,' said Dr John Masterson, head of the burns unit at Alfred Hospital in Melbourne, Australia. 'That lightning bolt was many, many thousands of volts.'

A hiker was scalped by a giant grizzly bear as his teenage daughter watched in horror. Johan Otter, 44, said he could feel the bear's teeth sink into his head and rip off his scalp, but his only concern was to protect his daughter, Jenna, from being savaged as well.

The two had been hiking in Glacier National Park, Montana, USA, when the mother bear, trying to protect her cubs, lunged at Johan. It sank its huge claws into his thigh and tossed him around. Johan curled into the foetal position but the bear climbed on top of him and bit into his skull.

A fraction deeper, and the fangs would have penetrated Johan's brain, said doctors. Johan miraculously escaped with 20 wounds, including a 'hangman's fracture' in the upper vertebrae, which is usually fatal.

One can only marvel at the survival of a 17-year-old American girl who spent 45 minutes under water. Carly Boohm was canoeing with friends in Wenatchee River in Washington State, USA, when the boat was sucked towards a bridge pillar by the force of the rushing waters. Her friends were thrown into the river and struggled to shore. But the canoe was wrapped around the pillar 'like tin foil' and Carly was pinned three feet under water.

'My lungs ached for air but I was trapped,' she recalled. 'I prayed that God would save me.'

Rescuers tried pulling the canoe away with a rope, but failed. Even a powerful motorboat couldn't battle the power of the river. By then, Carly had been under water for 25 minutes. A fire engine with a winch and cable was eventually able to lift the canoe away from Carly, whose body was immediately swept downriver. A volunteer raced after her in a motorboat and, by the time she was pulled out, Carly had been submerged for an unbelievable 45 minutes. Her heart had stopped and her body temperature had gone down to 72 degrees Fahrenheit. It was four days before she regained consciousness and two and a half months before she left hospital. She had to learn to speak, walk and read again, but went on to study to become a doctor.

'The fact that I am alive is a miracle,' she said.

Ari Schonbrun called a hurried 'goodbye' to his wife as he headed for the door to catch his train to work in New York City.

'You can't go until you've done Baruch's book order,' she told him sternly. He'd promised, but forgotten, to help his eight-year-old son choose some books from a catalogue by that day's deadline. Ari sighed and sat down for 20 minutes' haggling. It meant he missed his train, so it was after 8.40am when he arrived at his office building and took the lift to the 78th floor. As he got out and crossed to the next lift to take him to the 101st floor where he worked, American Airlines Flight 11 slammed into the skyscraper. It was 11 September 2001.

Above him, 658 of his colleagues were trapped. If Ari hadn't stopped to help his son and had arrived a few minutes earlier, he would have been among them. Instead, he managed to walk down the 78 flights to safety.

His miraculous escape has changed his outlook on life. 'My family comes first,' he said, 'and I don't run for buses or trains any more.'

Family and friends wept at Benjamin Maloney's memorial service. They mourned the

27-year-old Australian bush walker who had vanished in the Tasmanian wilderness.

But two weeks later, Maloney stunned them all when he stumbled, exhausted and emaciated, into a campsite.

What had started as a 12-day camping trip had turned into a 37-day ordeal in some of Australia's most inhospitable terrain. Without a sleeping bag, warm clothing or a compass, Maloney had endured weather conditions from scorching heat to frost. He'd stayed alive by drinking water and eating wild mushrooms, and had lost three stone by the end of the five weeks. After 18 days, police and rescue crews had given up hope of finding him alive and his parents arranged the memorial service.

'We can't believe he's back,' said his mother, Margaret. 'It's a miracle.'


Underwater photographer Valerie De La Valdene captured the shots of a lifetime – but they almost cost her life. Diving in the Galapagos Islands, she was filming a huge school of 10,000 fish when a large Galapagos shark started feeding on them.

'It was like hitting the jackpot,' she recalled.

Intent on becoming the first person ever to capture this feeding behaviour, Valerie didn't notice she was drifting away from the rest of her diving party, or that the big shark was eyeing up her, too, for his dinner. When she recognised the 'posturing' behaviour which signals attack, she surfaced rapidly but was horrified to discover the dive boat had gone. She was alone, surrounded by dozens of sharks, in the middle of an ocean that was whipping up 15-foot waves.

The six-foot-long sharks became increasingly aggressive, bumping and hitting her in frenzy while she tried to beat them off with her video camera.

'I started to scream terrifying guttural screams,' said Valerie. 'I was being eaten by sharks and knew I was going to die.'

In a last desperate bid for life, Valerie pushed her way through the sharks and started swimming towards a speck on the horizon she

14

prayed was land. For six hours she battled through the swells, repeating the childhood mantra of The Little Engine That Could – 'I think I can, I think I can.'

As she approached a tiny atoll, her exhausted body was sucked between two rocky pinnacles, which churned her around like a washing machine, mercilessly battering her against their jagged walls. A large wave eventually hauled her out and swept her into the rocks. Inch by inch, she crawled high enough to escape the waves and was eventually rescued when searchers saw the orange diving fin she used as a beacon.

Rob Gingery believes a miracle gave him a second chance at life. Depressed after his divorce and being separated from his son, he used his powerful motorcycle to push life to the limit, not caring whether or not he went over the edge.

One night he did go too far and ended up in a hospital in Memphis, Tennessee, with four skull fractures and broken limbs. Emergency surgery was performed after a massive blood clot formed in his brain and doctors warned he would be left a 'vegetable'.

His friends prayed by his bedside, willing him to live. No one could believe it when, just two and a half hours later, he regained consciousness and asked the nurse, 'What am I doing here?' He'd had brain surgery on the Monday and by Friday he was home. As well as an astounding physical recovery, Rob changed his entire outlook on life, starting his own business, but always wondering why he had been saved.

Almost a year to the day after his accident, as he was driving past the same intersection, two trucks collided in front of him. He rushed over and found a little girl, hanging upside down and unconscious, inside one of the vehicles. Her lips and skin were blue from the pressure of the seatbelt around her neck. The truck was leaking fluid and Rob was afraid it would explode before he could get the girl out.

He used a penknife to cut the seatbelt but didn't want to move her in case she had internal injuries. The only choice was to stay there until

16

the ambulance arrived and just hope the truck didn't catch fire.

It was a gamble that paid off, and, once the child was safe, Rob left the scene. He was later traced through the name on his penknife. The child's mother is sure Rob survived his accident in order to save her daughter.

It's the nightmare scenario for every parachutist. Kevin McIlwee, with his wife, Beverley, strapped to him for a tandem jump, pulled the cord – and the chute didn't open. The reserve chute opened only partially, so the newlyweds found themselves plunging helplessly 10,000 feet into the French countryside.

They hit the ground and, amazingly, both survived, although Kevin – a skydiving instructor and veteran of 4,500 jumps – suffered a badly broken leg.

Neva Howell knew she was taking a chance, speeding through torrential rain for an appointment. When she approached some roadworks, the traffic control light was green so she sped through the concrete retainers of the narrow lane at 50mph. Then the unthinkable happened. A large green car appeared in front of her and a head-on collision seemed inevitable.

The thought 'I am dead' flashed through her mind, but Neva finds it hard to explain what happened next. Instead of the horrendous crash she was expecting, Neva had the strangest experience of 'feeling' the other car slice through her own without actually making contact, and sensing the driver's body passing through hers.

'It's as if we merged at that moment,' she recalled. The next second, she was driving along again. When her consciousness registered what had happened, Neva stopped the car and cried hysterically.

'I couldn't explain away what happened with logic or analysis,' she said. 'It was a miracle.'

An Australian man built up a 40,000-volt charge of static electricity in his clothes as he walked, leaving a trail of scorched carpet and melting plastic. And he had no idea what was happening!

Frank Clewer, who was wearing a woollen shirt and a nylon jacket, was oblivious to the growing electrical current caused by his clothes rubbing together. When he walked into a building in Victoria, he heard loud cracking sounds and scorch marks appeared over the carpet. The fire brigade was called and the building evacuated.

When Clewer returned to his car and noticed the plastic on the floor had melted, he went to see fire official Henry Barton who tested Clewer's clothes and measured the amazingly high current. If it had been any higher, it would have ignited his clothing.

'In 35 years of firefighting, I've never come across anything like this,' said Barton. 'He's a lucky man to have escaped unhurt.'


Experts estimate human survival time without food and water at no more than a week, so it's not surprising that the discovery of a 19-year-old girl, buried alive for 16 days after a building collapsed, was hailed a miracle in South Korea.

More than 500 people died in 1995 when the busy five-storey department store fell down in Seoul, trapping 1,500 shoppers. Sales assistant Park Seung-Hyun was the last to be pulled alive from the rubble, to the disbelief of her rescuers.

Stephen Hearn was dragged from the wreck of his car after it had ploughed through trees into a ditch – and he was still asleep!

The 41-year-old computer analyst was pulled to safety by a passer-by, who thought it odd the driver was barefoot and, despite having suffered serious injuries, that Stephen still hadn't woken up.

He was cleared of dangerous driving after Warwick Crown Court heard he had a condition that caused him to sleepwalk regularly. Doctors told him the only reason he was alive was because his body had been so relaxed in sleep.

'I don't remember anything about that night after I'd dozed off in the living room,' said

Stephen. 'I know I'm lucky to be alive. The car was a write-off, and I could have been one too!'

Maralyn and Maurice Bailey boarded their 31-foot yacht in Southampton and set off in high spirits for a new life in New Zealand.

As they approached the coast of Guatemala, they collided with a huge whale, which rammed a gaping hole in their hull. They were forced to abandon ship taking whatever supplies they could get into their tiny rubber dinghy. Little did they realise that this was to be their home for 117 harrowing days adrift.

The Baileys ate raw turtle, seabirds and fish they caught with their bare hands. As the weeks turned into months, their clothes rotted on their bodies and they developed painful sores from sunburn and salt water. The dinghy, too, was deteriorating. It overturned three times during heavy storms and was constantly buffeted by sharks.

As death beckoned the Baileys' battered bodies, a miracle saved them. The crew of a Korean fishing boat already off-course after a fishing expedition, altered course to investigate the curious small blob they'd spotted on the horizon.

The couple were hauled, semi-conscious, aboard the Korean vessel and slowly nursed back to health by the kindly crew, who massaged the couple's limbs until movement returned.

A super-fit soldier was given 48 hours to live after he dropped 1,000 feet like a stone when his parachutes failed to open.

Alan Craven, 23, was badly injured but survived thanks to his superb physique, said doctors. The bulging muscles took the impact when he hit the ground at 120 mph during a training exercise in North Carolina, USA.

The record for surviving the longest fall without a parachute is held by Yugoslavian airhostess Vesna Vulovic, who plunged 33,330 feet over the Czech Republic when a plane exploded in 1972.

It was the second miracle for Guy Tozzoli, President of the World Trade Center's Association, when he was held up for 45 minutes by an accident on his way into the city. He arrived just as United Airlines Flight 175 crashed into Tower 2.

In 1993, he had cheated death by arriving at work early and parking his car only minutes before a bomb exploded, killing six people in the garage.

'People in my office call me The Cat because they swear I must have nine lives,' said Tozzoli.


A pleasant day's cycling on their favourite trail turned into a nightmare for friends Debi Nichols and Anne Hjelle.

They planned to do a short loop through parkland in the Santa Monica Mountains, California. Half an hour later, as they sped down a hill, Anne saw a flash of movement over her right shoulder. The next thing she knew was that she'd been knocked off her bike and some kind of animal had grabbed the back of her head. It was a puma, which had already tasted

23

human blood that day; the body of a cyclist was lying in a deep ravine.

Now the animal had sunk its deadly teeth into Anne's flesh and went on biting her as she struggled to hit it in the face. Debi arrived and threw her bike, hoping to scare the beast off. But it held on to Anne and started to drag her down the hillside. Debi lunged and caught her friend's leg so the puma couldn't carry her off.

This tug of war went on while a fang broke Anne's nose and the other fang went into her upper lip. When the puma closed its powerful jaws over her face, she felt her cheek tearing away. Anne knew she was staring death in the face. Suddenly, two cyclists who had heard Debi's screams for help started pelting the puma with rocks. Eventually, it let go of Anne and ran into the bushes. Anne was rushed to hospital in a critical condition, with more than 30 bite wounds to the front of her neck, a mauled eye and facial nerve damage.

'That animal was totally capable of killing me but I'm here to tell the tale,' said Anne, who required considerable reconstructive surgery.

She even cycles the same trail where she almost lost her life.

It was a normal hectic morning in the Tafoya household as Judy and Lincoln were helping nanny Angel Garcia get the couple's six children ready. As soon as Lincoln left to take five of the children to school, Judy sat at her computer to email credit card orders for the family business.

As the vehicle pulled out of the driveway, three-year-old Chelsea ran past Angel and out of the door to try and catch up with her father. Angel watched, horrified, as the little girl, failing to reach the door handle, jumped on to the truck's back bumper. Angel shouted for Judy to call the police, but the phone line was tied up by the credit card transactions and she couldn't dial out. Meanwhile, Lincoln was racing to get his children to school on time, unaware his baby daughter was hanging on for dear life. Another driver, Connie Romero, spotted Chelsea and tried to get Lincoln's attention by flashing her lights and honking her horn.

Lincoln accelerated away from what he assumed was road rage and tried to lose the driver. Connie feared Chelsea would fall off and fly through her windscreen or be run over by her. In a desperate last bid to get Lincoln to stop, she sped up to prevent him overtaking and stayed alongside him until he looked over and realised what she wanted.

But, when they pulled over and looked, Chelsea had gone. They found her at the front of the truck, cold but otherwise unharmed.

'It had to be a miracle for a little kid like that to hang on going that fast and hitting that many bumps,' said Lincoln.

Helen Kelly's bra gave her more support than she'd ever dreamed of when the underwire deflected a stray bullet.

Helen, 24, was caught in a shoot-out between rival gangs outside London's Barbican Centre. She escaped almost certain death when a bullet glanced off the wire, hitting her right breast instead of her heart.

'It's great to be late' has become lawyer Rick Filkins's motto since 9/11.

On the way to his office in the New York Stock Exchange, Rick stopped to vote in the local elections. When he discovered that his registration paper was missing, he almost shrugged it off and kept going. Instead, he spent 20 minutes completing a form, which enabled him to cast his ballot.

By the time he caught his train, Flight 11 had hit Tower 1, where he should have been.

Search and Rescue boats cruising the flooded streets of New Orleans after Hurricane Katrina had all but given up hope of finding anyone alive after 18 days.

Then they heard a faint cry: 'Hey, over here.' They broke into the little wooden house and found 76-year-old Gerald Martin sitting in a chair in his sludge-covered kitchen. He had spent the first 16 days of his ordeal in his attic, in which temperatures soared dangerously high; then had gone downstairs when the waters had subsided.

He had had no food and had run out of water. Rescuers said he couldn't have lasted much longer.

Stuart Hillman is lucky to be alive after he fell from a railway bridge on to electric cables carrying 24,000 volts.

He suffered serious burns to his legs, arms and face when he plunged from the bridge over the Wolverhampton to Birmingham main line in Coseley, Dudley, England.

A Bavarian builder had a miraculous escape when he was speared through the neck by a pneumatic drill.

Harry Moeller, 49, was working on the foundations of a new garage at his home near Munich when the machine slipped, somersaulted from his hands and the two-inch drill bit stabbed him through his neck. When his wife, Karen, arrived with his lunch, the machine was still running with the deadly metal drill embedded in Harry's neck.

He was airlifted to hospital where doctors expected him to make a full recovery.

Astrid Oates and her unborn child survived death by inches when a wooden stake pierced her breast in a road accident.

She was a passenger in a car that careered off the road in Axminster, Devon, and smashed through a heavy wooden fence. One post sliced past Astrid, who was eight months pregnant, but a second shattered before impaling her. She was aware that a piece of wood was sticking out of her body as rescuers spent 70 minutes cutting her free from the wreckage.

It took surgeons four hours to remove the stake, which doctors said was dangerously close to her heart.

Katzi Carver has the rest of her life to thank the man who rescued her from the brink of suicide – she married him.

One desperate night, Katzi checked into a motel in Dallas, Texas, and swallowed a handful of pills. At 3am, her friend, Bo Carver, woke from a deep sleep and got out of bed for no reason. He had a bad feeling about Katzi so he called her house. Her son had no idea where she was so Bo set off on the hour's drive to Katzi's house.

On the way, he drove past a Ramada Inn and something made him pull in and circle the car park three times until he spotted Katzi's car. The motel manager was reluctant to open Katzi's door but Bo persuaded him, explaining that it was an emergency. When they broke in, they found Katzi lying unconscious, surrounded by empty bottles. She was rushed to hospital just in time.

'So many things had to come together to have made this happen,' said Katzi. 'If they hadn't, I wouldn't be alive today.

'And we wouldn't have fallen in love and got married.'

Toddler Connor McCombe defied doctors' grim prognoses and survived being run over by a fully loaded semi-trailer.

He ran out to greet the driver, whom he knew, but the driver didn't see him and reversed over the boy. Connor almost bled to death before he reached hospital in Melbourne, Australia, where he spent three months. Doctors said the accident would have killed any adult, but Connor was saved because he had young, flexible bones.

Maria Tejada believes she owes her life to her dead father. She was relaxing in her Florida home when she was stunned to hear his voice urgently warning her to get off the couch immediately. Instinctively, she leaped off her seat and ran to the next room – just as a speeding car smashed through the wall and ploughed into the sofa where she'd been sitting.

'If I hadn't listened to my father, I'd be dead,' said the relieved mother of six. 'I'm the luckiest person in the world.' Maria's father had died five years earlier from cancer. But, when she heard his voice that day, it sounded as though he was in the room with her.

'I was shaking like a leaf,' said Maria. 'I thought I was dreaming when he spoke.'

Marianne McInerney, executive director of the National Business Travel Association, was booked on American Airlines Flight 77 on 11 September 2001, but she changed her ticket to a cheaper one with United Airlines.

It was the most important decision of her life. Flight 77 crashed into the Pentagon, but her plane landed safely.

US Coastguards, searching the Caribbean for a missing schooner, flew towards a tiny speck they'd spotted in the water. It was a woman, clinging desperately to a piece of corrugated steel no bigger than a door. She lifted an arm and waved feebly in a last-ditch attempt to be saved.

The crew had no idea how she had drifted 80 miles north of the Honduran mainland, but they radioed the British frigate Sheffield for help and an hour later the woman was winched aboard.

For a while she lapsed in and out of consciousness and her blood pressure and temperature were dangerously low. As she recovered, she told her rescuers that her house had been destroyed by floodwater and she had been swept into the sea with her husband and three children. She had been drifting for six days and survived 25-30-foot waves whipped up by Hurricane Mitch.

'It was absolutely amazing that she came through an ordeal like that,' said Commander Colin Hamp.

For some reason three is often considered to be a lucky number. It certainly was for two Irish policemen in Dublin.

A masked gunman fired at them THREE times at point-blank range, but each time the gun jammed. Officers Ian Lambe and Fergal McDonagh then arrested the gunman and his accomplice at an off-licence.

A motorist who had a heart attack was brought back from the dead – by his seatbelt!

Conn Castell, aged 65, of Reading, Berkshire, England, collapsed at the wheel and his car veered across the road and into a hedge. The impact of the crash tugged the belt so sharply across his chest that the jolt restarted his heart.

Brenda Archer and her family were settling down to a quiet evening in front of the television when they had an unexpected visitor from outer space. A grapefruit-sized meteorite smashed through the roof of their home in Auckland, New Zealand, narrowly missing Brenda's one-year-old grandson.

The four-and-a-half-billion-year-old, 2.9lb piece of space junk was travelling at an estimated

300mph when it crashed into the home, bouncing off the couch before hitting the ceiling.

Experts say the chances of a house being hit by a meteorite are billions to one.

Surfer Hoku Aki knew his time was up. His leg was firmly clamped between the powerful jaws of a killer shark, which was dragging him under the water.

Hoku wrestled with the shark, trying to prise its razor teeth off his foot, but it was futile. He prepared himself for death. Suddenly, he saw the shark's eye open, so he jabbed his finger into the eye and tore it from its socket.

The shark fled in pain and, despite losing his foot, Hoku swam 60 feet back to shore in Honolulu, Hawaii. Today, he can tell a 'the one that got away' tale to beat all others!

A British student in Israel, shot in the head by her boyfriend's killer, escaped death by a hair's breadth.

35

The gunman's bullet hit Charlotte Gibb's face just in front of her right ear and came out fractionally below her left eye. Incredibly, it missed every vital nerve. If the trajectory had been a millimetre one way or another, it would have gone straight into her brain and killed her.

'It must be a million-to-one to be shot through the face and not have serious repercussions,' said Mr David Adlam, facial surgeon at Addenbrooke's Hospital, Cambridge. 'She hasn't even lost a tooth, let alone suffered any facial paralysis.'

$A$t the end of their idyllic family camping holiday, Debbie Evans went home with her baby daughter to let husband, Mike, have an extra day's uninterrupted fishing.

On a glorious morning in the middle of Lake Travis near Austin, Texas, Mike bent down to untangle his fishing line and accidentally swivelled his seat. It hit the back of the tiller handle on the outboard motor and the boat turned sharply, propelling Mike into the water.

He struggled to get back into the boat but it was turning in swift circles around him. Then it suddenly took off, leaving Mike floundering in a hundred feet of water, a thousand feet from shore and without a life jacket.

He tried to swim to the bank but realised halfway across that he wasn't going to make it. His leg was injured and he felt himself slipping helplessly under the water as exhaustion overtook him.

Mike said silent goodbyes to his wife and daughter and resigned himself to death. As he made one last effort to break the surface of the water, he saw a boat speeding towards him. It was his boat and, for one horrifying moment, Mike thought it had come back to finish him off! Then he saw two men on board, who helped him out of the water.

Mike discovered that the propeller blades had shredded his shorts and torn three large gashes in his leg. He also discovered from his rescuers the bizarre behaviour of his boat. After it had straightened out from its spin, it had headed a quarter of a mile down the lake before making an inexplicable 90-degree turn into the country club harbour. It drove past dozens of expensive yachts and pleasure boats without touching any of them, then turned left again to crash into the bank just below where the two men were doing an unscheduled day's construction work on a waterfront house.

'If that boat hadn't made its miraculous trip to the shore, I would have drowned in the lake,' said Mike. 'I think an angel must have been at the helm.'

Computer programmer Tom Maciejewski stayed up late on 10 September to watch a football game. He couldn't get up on time the next morning and by the time he got into the city his office building was engulfed in flames.

'What if I'd fallen asleep watching that game? What if I'd woken up early and got to work on time? What if I'd had a meeting there I couldn't miss?'

Tom never stops asking himself the 'What if?' question.

The annual weekend ski trip called 'Snow Madness' has been renamed 'Snow Miracle' by Californian friends David Moss and Dennis Eucalyptus.

On the first night of their expedition, the weather on Mount Lassen changed unexpectedly and they woke to heavy snowfall around their tents. They decided to head back, but the blizzard was disorientating. In the severe weather, with no tracks to follow, they found themselves heading into avalanche territory. Dennis was leading the way, while David followed, closely watching his footfalls in the deep snow. Suddenly Dennis disappeared. He had sunk without trace into an avalanche.

'He was somewhere under me, dying,' recalls David. 'I knew that, if I didn't reach him within 30 minutes, it would be too late.'

Although David was able to call for help on his mobile phone, it was four hours before rescuers found them. In the meantime, David stuck his skis into the ground in the shape of an X, the international symbol for distress, and began digging frantically in the snow.

Two hours later, he was feeling weak and beginning to suffer from hypothermia. He was also in despair, certain that his friend of 20 years was dead. When the rescuers arrived, they used probes and a search dog in a last-ditch attempt to locate Dennis – or, at least, his body.

Then they found a glove. Reluctantly, they pulled and discovered it was still on Dennis's hand and, to their amazement, they could hear soft moaning from beneath the snow. Defying all the laws, Dennis had survived five and a half hours buried under nearly six feet of snow. He recovered quickly in hospital, with no evidence of frostbite.

'I was absolutely astonished that he was so intact,' said Dr Dana Ware. 'There is no scientific explanation for this. What happened to him was a miracle.'

Despite the warning on the packet, smoking has actually saved a life.

Seconds after a receptionist in an Irish office

nipped out to have a ciggy, a car careered across the road and smashed through the window into the spot where she'd been sitting.

At first the car looked empty, but stunned eyewitnesses discovered two terrified young children strapped into their seats in the back. Their mother had forgotten to apply the handbrake when she'd parked the car.

Road workers repairing a guard rail above a Southern California canyon climbed down to explore a car wreck 300 feet below.

They couldn't believe their eyes when they found five-year-old Ruby Bustamante sitting inside the car beside her dead mother, Norma. The child had not only survived the fatal impact, but had also been stranded down there for ten days, living on dry noodles and a can of drink she'd found in the wreck. The car had skidded off the motorway and into the isolated canyon about 90 miles southeast of Los Angeles, in an area frequented by coyotes and pumas.

Asian tsunami survivor Ari Afrizal refused to let the sea swallow him along with the thousands who perished.

He clung to life in the middle of the ocean for two weeks after being sucked from the stricken land. After swimming and floating for an hour, 22-year-old Ari clambered on to a wooden plank that had drifted by along with bloated bodies.

After seven days, when he was giving up hope of rescue, he found an abandoned boat which gave him shelter from the searing sun, and watched from its deck as sharks circled expectantly.

On the fifteenth day, a container ship spotted him about 75 miles from the nearest island and pulled him aboard. Ari had survived at sea longer than any tsunami victim.

Toddler Liam Evans survived for three days by eating soil after his granddad's car crashed down a mountainside.

The car had plunged 150 yards down the slope and somersaulted before coming to rest, killing retired policeman Gwilym Evans. Thirteen-month-old Liam, who had been freed from the wreckage on impact, kept warm by covering himself in ferns and kept alive by getting moisture from the soil he ate.

A ten-year-old picnicker discovered Liam when he heard him crying.

A Scottish man flattened by a three-ton road roller can't believe he's alive to tell the tale. Andy Duffy, 46, knows he should have been squashed to a pulp as the heavy machine ran over him from head to foot and crushed him into the road.

To the doctors' amazement, he suffered only a broken leg, shattered ribs and smashed facial bones.

All 309 passengers aboard an Air France jet somehow survived when the plane crash-landed at Toronto Airport and burst into flames seconds later.

The Airbus skidded off the end of the

runway, crashed through barriers skirting Canada's busiest motorway and ended up in a ravine. Black smoke and flames filled the cabins as terrified passengers leaped from the plane and ran for their lives. Within three minutes, the Airbus was emptied and, just 90 seconds later, it was enveloped in fire.

'It's incredible, a miracle,' said Canada's Transport Minister Jean Lapierre.

Jonathan Waldick's parents feared the worst when a 200mph tornado sucked the toddler from the bedroom of his Florida home.

The 18-month-old was asleep when the twister ripped through the state, killing 39 people. The ferocious winds flattened his family's home in Kissimmee and when rescuers went in search of Jonathan they found his bedroom was just a pile of rubble.

An hour later, as they were giving up hope, one of them spotted a foot among the tangled branches. Jonathan was curled up on his mattress, wide-eyed with fright but safe and sound.

Language assistant Conor Aiken took a day off work — and escaped the horrific Madrid train bombings that killed 70 people.

Conor, 21, would normally have been standing at Atocha station waiting to catch his train at the time a blast shattered the area.

Instead, he was escorting pupils to a careers conference, a change of plan that saved the Irishman's life.

A 65-year-old woman had a miraculous escape when she was thrown from a bus, which then rolled down an embankment and landed on top of her.

Lucy Bate, from Warrington in Cheshire, England, suffered only a head injury and a broken ankle after the bus collided with a car and veered across the road into a crash barrier. It then hit a tree before toppling over the barrier and rolling 30 feet down an embankment. Mrs Bate hurtled from the vehicle, only to be trapped beneath it when it landed.

Several passengers levered the bus away from

her and propped it on bricks until firefighters arrived to free her.

Injured and alone, 4,500 feet up a mountain-top in Alaska, Mike Harbaugh waited for certain death.

The remains of his Cessna plane lay scattered around the summit of Merill Pass and he was crouched in the remains of the fuselage, freezing and in great pain. His eyes had frozen shut and his ankle and collarbone seemed to be broken. He managed to melt enough snow to take sips of water every hour or so, but after three days in the sub-zero February weather, he was growing rapidly weaker.

Unbeknown to Mike, a massive air search was under way to find him. It involved the risky tactic of a plane flying over the pass and dropping huge flares every few minutes in order to provide sufficient light for the helicopter below to navigate through the narrow gap.

The chopper's crew were putting their own lives in danger; if the flares went out, they would fly into the black canyon walls. But they managed to reach Mike and raced against time to stretcher him out. He had lost 30lb and his core body temperature was down to below 80 degrees Fahrenheit, one of the lowest ever recorded in a patient who survived.

Although doctors had to amputate one leg, Mike thanks a miracle for making him the first crash victim to come away from that summit alive.

Commuters gasped in horror as they watched a toddler plummet 23 feet from a railway footbridge on to a concrete platform below.

Shannon Monahan, aged three, fell through the gap left by a missing panel at Galton Bridge station in Smethwick, Birmingham, England, but somehow escaped without serious injuries.

'I don't know how she survived,' said her mother, Jennifer.

If Helen Monahan's friend hadn't phoned asking her to pick up her children from school, she would have still been inside her house when a light aircraft crashed into the roof.

By leaving early to help out her friend, Helen's life, and possibly her children's, was spared. Minutes later, they would have been playing in the garden where the plane toppled after hitting the three-bedroom house in Shoreham-by-Sea, West Sussex.

The pilot also escaped, with only minor injuries.

In the early hours of the morning, Lana Hudspeth lost control of her car, hit a tree, fell down a 30-foot embankment and ended up on the railway track. The accident could have killed her. Two hours later, a train came along and slammed into the car, pushing it 300 yards down the track. She still didn't die.

Unbelievably, 37-year-old Lana was still alive when the emergency services arrived and airlifted her to hospital near Columbia, Missouri, USA.

'Given the amount of force from that crash, I

would say it was a miracle that someone survived it,' said Highway Patrolman Bryan McDougal.

A 22-year-old backpacker from Nuneaton can't explain why she hesitated asking for the bill in a Bali restaurant, but those precious few minutes bought her life.

Hayley Dewis knew that she was 45 minutes late for meeting friends in Paddy's Bar, but, even when the waitress brought fresh fruit at the end of the meal and she noticed it was 10.45pm, Hayley didn't ask her for the bill.

'Had I paid then, I'd have been outside and probably at Paddy's when the bomb went off at 11pm,' she said. 'Something made me hesitate.'

Alice Brooking was tempted to have a short nap before she met the group of musicians she was to accompany round Paris.

Instead, she decided to kill those 15 minutes by chatting to her sister, Natalie, in London. Suddenly, the room shook violently and over the phone Natalie heard an enormous bang. Alice dropped the phone and opened her door to find the landing engulfed in flames. Thick black smoke filled the room, choking her, and the heat was intense. By chance, Alice had opened her first-floor window before she'd made the call to her sister. Now it was her only hope of escape as the flames licked closer.

Urged by the hotel receptionist standing on the ground below, Alice jumped and he broke her fall with his body. Then Alice just ran, and kept on running barefoot across a field to the main road. She looked back and saw a massive wall of flame, and discovered that Concorde had crashed on her hotel.

The modern languages undergraduate from Tonbridge in Kent, England, knows her life was saved because she had been awake when the plane came down. Had she decided to sleep, she would have been burned alive.

'The more I learned about what happened, the more I realise it truly is a miracle I survived,' she said.

It was like a scene from a nail-biting movie. A car flies off the road, over an embankment and lands on the railway track. The driver's trapped and a train's approaching.

This was the stark reality for Eunice and Shaun Meyers, who were on their way to the shops in Beltsville, Maryland, USA, when the car flew by. While Eunice called the emergency services, Shaun dashed to the car where an elderly couple sat injured and distressed. They begged him to stay with them until the paramedics arrived so Shaun held the old lady's hand and tried to comfort the couple.

But then he heard someone shout, 'The train's coming.' The old man was helped to safety by two passers-by but the old woman had her seatbelt wrapped around her arm and hand. Shaun could feel the vibrations of the approaching train but he stayed and worked methodically to free the woman's arms. He pulled her from the wreckage seconds before the locomotive demolished the car.

'I could hear everyone screaming for me to get out, but what could I do?' said Shaun, a 42-

year-old construction-firm owner. 'I wasn't going to leave her.'

$A$ Sri Lankan couple have no doubt that they were saved from the Asian tsunami by a higher power.

Sumith Doluweera's in-laws went to church as usual on the morning of the disaster, but that day the service ran ten minutes late. Had they walked home earlier, they would have perished in the waves, along with their neighbours.

$C$anadian pilot Al Walls was just two minutes from disaster when his plane ran out of fuel over the Atlantic. He was delivering the brand-new aircraft to a Dutch customer but, halfway through the flight, he realised he had a fuel leak. His auxiliary pump had failed so he couldn't transfer fuel from there.

Al decided it was better to continue his journey than to turn back into a headwind, and he just hoped he'd reach some land before he ran out of fuel completely. He managed to limp towards Shannon Airport, then he taxied down the runway as the aircraft's single engine spluttered to a halt on the last drop of fuel.

At 9.30 every morning, toddlers at a nursery in New Jersey, USA, gather for 'Circle Time' on the blue rug in the centre of the main room.

One Wednesday, breakfast had been later than usual and the pre-schoolers were still washing their hands a few minutes after 9.30am. Suddenly, there was a huge screech, followed by a big boom, and a car crashed through the wall and into the room, filling it with smoke and the smell of burning rubber. The vehicle splintered desks and bookcases in its path, before landing in the middle of the blue rug with its wheels spinning.

'Normally, that's where all the children would have been sitting,' said teacher Tonya Williamson. 'And that's where they sleep at naptime. Someone was protecting those kids that day.'

US Fire Captain Ed Cushing woke in a sweat from a vivid nightmare. He'd been called to a house fire where neighbours told him two children and their mother were trapped. Feeling his way through the dense smoke and ferocious heat, he located the mother, who was unconscious, and carried her outside where he administered CPR. He went back into the blazing building and rescued a child, but he knew there was another one in there. Again he battled the inferno and, as he brought out the second child, his chief congratulated him on a good job.

A few hours later, Ed was on duty for real when an alarm came in for a major house fire. No one knew how many people there were on the first floor so Ed rushed inside, kicked down the door and carried an unconscious woman to safety.

He managed to get her heart restarted using CPR, then raced back to search for more survivors. When he brought out a small boy, he realised that he was living his dream and he was the only one who knew there would be a second child in the building. Remembering the layout from his dream, he crawled up the stairs on his stomach and went straight to the boy's body.

Ed pushed the toddler's chest and breathed into his face as he ran from the flames, and the boy's heart started beating. And, just as he had been in the dream, Ed's chief was there to thank him. This time, though, the chief said he didn't think the mother and the little boy were going to survive.

'Oh, yes, they will,' said Ed confidently.

# CHAPTER TWO:
# Medical Marvels

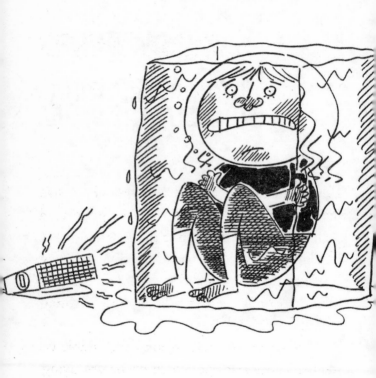

# MEDICAL MARVELS

Flying doctor Heather Clark brought a stab victim back from the dead when she performed open-heart surgery on a pub floor.

Stephen Niland had been knifed in the chest in an East London bar and was lying on the floor when Heather and her colleague, Alistair Mulcahy, arrived.

Although only a small wound was visible on Stephen's chest, Heather could see he was dying. She had to act quickly, first by checking to make sure the knife hadn't punctured a lung. But, when she realised he had no pulse, and was clinically dead, Heather knew her only option was to open up his chest and apply pressure to the heart. There were just three minutes before his brain – starved of oxygen – would cease to function.

Using scissors designed to cut off patients' clothes, Heather struggled to slice through Stephen's flesh to the breastbone. Alistair used clamps to prise open the chest wall like a clamshell while Heather probed the bloody gap to reach the heart. With skilled and certain hands, she cut the sac around the organ to scoop out a blood clot, which would have proved fatal.

Stephen's heart was restarted with gentle massage, but blood began spurting from the knife wound. The only solution was for Alistair to plug the hole with his forefinger, which he kept there until Stephen reached the hospital where surgeons applied 70 stitches to the wound.

He was discharged six days later, after a visit from Heather who was hailed a miracle worker.

When a landmine ripped nine-year-old Saleh Khalaf's body apart, medics waited for the inevitable. His abdomen had been torn open, his left eye was missing and both hands had been blown off.

Dr Jay Johannigman, a surgeon and veteran of two Gulf wars, had never seen anyone live through such horrific injuries. Yet, when the boy whispered a request for water, Johannigman, who knew his job was to treat only American soldiers, couldn't give up the faint hope of saving Saleh.

The boy, whose brother had died when Saleh picked up the landmine on an Iraqi street, had been taken to a hospital in Nasiriya, 50 miles away, after the accident. With limited facilities, doctors had stitched his organs back into place and put bandages over his mangled forearms, then waited for him to die.

A doctor advised his father, Raheem, that the child's only chance was to be taken to the Americans who were in the country as part of Operation Iraqi Freedom in 2003. Raheem went to the airbase and, in pidgin English and sign language, managed to convey his story to the soldiers.

61

Dr Johannigman went with the ambulance to pick up Saleh but, when he was able to examine the boy, hope faded. The stitches holding his colon, stomach, liver and small intestine had burst apart with the swelling of his organs, and gangrene was spreading inside his abdomen.

Against the rules – and his better judgement – the doctor operated ten times in the next eight hours. He even used a plastic IV bag to close Saleh's abdomen because there wasn't enough skin to cover it. But, after each surgery, the boy would wake up and ask for food. Johannigman had never seen such resilience.

Saleh hovered between life and death as his father, nurses and doctors prayed around his bedside. In the middle of the night, it seemed the prayers had been heard. The heavy bleeding stopped and Saleh, the strong survivor, was given the nickname 'Lion Heart'.

His story touched the hearts of Americans and donations flooded in. The Children's Hospital Oakland, California, agreed to treat him free of charge and Saleh was airlifted there for more surgery and lengthy rehabilitation.

The miracle that gave Margie Levine a second chance at life continues to bring healing to other cancer victims.

When the 43-year-old American health education teacher and social worker was given six months to live following a diagnosis with pleural mesothelomia, a deadly lung cancer caused by asbestos exposure, she refused to give up despite confirmation of the grim prognosis by three medical centres.

Doctors in Boston, Massachusetts, advised her to forgo treatment and live out her remaining months with dignity. At first, she agreed and went home to organise her will, give away her favourite possessions and see old friends. But, driven by a remarkable tenacity, Margie started researching her disease and drew up a plan to fight it. She persuaded her doctors to follow the radical and unconventional course of major surgery involving the removal of the tumour and part of her lung, rebuilding her chest wall and placing 100 metal clips around her heart, followed by four chemo sessions and 25 radiation treatments.

Then Margie immersed herself in a range of complementary medicine practices, including meditation, acupuncture and a vegetable diet. She astounded her doctors by going on to become the longest survivor of the disease. Her case was studied at Harvard Medical School and her methods are being employed in hospitals and clinics worldwide.

Sarah Yeargain watched in horror and disbelief as the skin started to peel off her whole body. As her terrified mother, Katherine, carried her 29-year-old daughter into the hospital, she felt sheets of skin coming off on to her hands. The young American was suffering an extreme allergic reaction to a commonly prescribed antibiotic for a sinus infection.

Doctors in San Diego gave Sarah no chance of survival as the skin disappeared from her entire body, including her scalp and the membranes covering her mouth, eyes and throat. Without skin, she had no protection from infection. Medics told her mother they feared Sarah would have a heart attack from the pain.

'Generally with a hundred per cent skin loss, there's a hundred per cent mortality,' said Mrs Yeargain.

Sarah's life was saved with the use of an amazing artificial skin called TransCyte, which was stapled all over her body to create a seal and stop infection. After a few weeks it dissolved as new skin emerged.

'It's a miracle. I can't think of any other word to describe what happened,' said her grandmother. 'Sarah went from the brink of death to being back home in just three weeks.'

A summer boat trip turned to tragedy when 18-year-old Jacob Brochtrup's leg was mangled in the propeller. The wound was so massive that Jacob lost almost all the blood in his body, causing his heart to stop. Emergency medics went through the motions of saving their patient, even though he had no pulse, no brain function, no heartbeat and he wasn't breathing. In short, the situation looked hopeless.

When Jacob arrived at Brackenridge Hospital, Texas, he was clinically dead as he had been in cardiac arrest for at least 45 minutes. Trauma surgeon Dr John Uecker and physician Tracey Weir were ready to pronounce death. Following standard procedure they checked one more time for a pulse and, to their astonishment, detected a faint beat.

Though still doubtful of Jacob's chances of survival, Uecker ordered massive amounts of blood to replace what had been lost in the lake, and pumped in medications. He reviewed the injuries to Jacob's leg, which had been twisted around 360 degrees. All the quadriceps muscle and major blood vessels had been cut, and the thighbone was broken in two. There was no way it could be saved.

An hour later, the surgeon performed his first-ever amputation from the hip, warning Jacob's parents that, even if their son survived the surgery, it was unlikely his brain would be normal.

Jacob was given hypothermia therapy in

which his body was cooled to help preserve his brain function, an unconventional treatment that worked for him. On the day he was moved out of Intensive Care, an MRI showed that his brain was normal and undamaged. This was confirmed when Jacob, sitting up in bed eating breakfast one morning, greeted Uecker cheerily, 'Hey, dude. How's it going?'

Despite pneumonia and leg infections, he made a full recovery and was given a prosthesis by a local hospital.

'I really think we witnessed a miracle in this case,' said Uecker.


Mary Self had just three weeks to live. She was just 34 years old, and dying from a tumour on her spine. Though no stranger to cancer, Mary grieved for the husband and two children she would leave behind. She chose her funeral hymns and wrote letters to her son, Adam, and daughter, Bethany, to be opened after her death.

Then one day she received an unexpected

telephone call. Specialists at the Royal Orthopaedic Hospital in Birmingham, England, noticed from her most recent scan that the tumour appeared to be shrinking. Three weeks later, it had disappeared altogether!

It was the culmination of some miraculous events in Mary's life, starting with the first diagnosis of cancer when she was 17. Told that her only, albeit slim, hope of survival was amputation above the knee and chemotherapy, the plucky teen agreed and, incredibly, survived.

Mary went on to enter medical school where she met her husband, Richard, and they both qualified as doctors. She was thrilled but surprised when she became pregnant twice, because she thought the chemo had left her infertile. But inoperable cancer soon returned in her lung and spine and the prognosis was terminal. All the doctors could do was to provide pain control.

Mary and Richard decided the only thing left to try was prayer and, for the next five months, friends and family prayed intensively for Mary's recovery. It worked.

'The doctors were amazed and asked if I had any explanation,' she said. 'I told them it was a miracle and the specialist said he would buy that.'

No one can explain what made little Jack Feast's heart start to beat normally hours before a risky transplant operation.

But his South London parents, Nick and Sue, have no doubt that it was a miracle. Their six-year-old son had been born with a hole in the heart but, after surgery was performed to repair it, Jack showed no signs of recovery. He was hooked up to a sophisticated life support machine and for 11 days he hovered on the brink of death while his family kept a bedside vigil.

With every passing day, doctors knew his chances were diminishing as no other child had survived for more than seven days on the machine. By the time a donor heart had been located in the Czech Republic, they feared the boy's heart would be too weak to cope with the operation.

But when nurses took him off the machine in readiness for surgery, everyone was astounded to find Jack's heart was beating on its own. The transplant was never performed and Jack was sent home to lead a normal life.

'Jack definitely defied all the odds,' said Dr David Anderson, 'but we don't know how or why.'

Turning to the internet for answers is often useful, but for Alex Lowe it was life saving. The eight-year-old, who suffers from a genetic immune deficiency disorder, lapsed into a coma after being paralysed with five brain tumours. She was given hours to live and a priest was called to administer the last rites.

In a desperate bid to save Alex, her parents persuaded a doctor to try an experimental therapy that a friend had read about on the internet that, according to scientists at Edinburgh University, could boost the immune system.

Consultant haematologist Robert Wynn, at the Royal Manchester Children's Hospital, agreed to try the treatment and within weeks

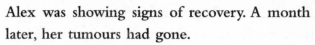
Alex was showing signs of recovery. A month later, her tumours had gone.

'She was in a deep coma, very close to death,' said Dr Wynn. 'It's not too much to describe what happened as miraculous. I've never seen anything like it.'

The world's largest tumour weighed a mind-boggling 14 stone and took 18 hours and 50 pints of blood for surgeons to remove it.

The patient, Lori Hoogewind, suffered from neurofibromatosis, which causes small, usually benign, tumours to grow on the body. She had had several of these removed before a malignant tumour was found.

Lori, who lives in Michigan, USA, was given radiotherapy, which stopped the tumour but had a catastrophic side-effect: an explosion of tissue growth. Within a few months the tumour had ballooned to 14 stone and wrapped itself around her from her back to her stomach.

Death seemed inevitable until a team of expert medics took on the challenge to save

Lori's life. Halfway through the operation, major problems arose and things looked grim. If they continued, Lori could die, but to stop would kill her too. They decided to go on. Ultimately, the operation was a success and went into the annals of medical history.

After a devastating house fire, which left her burned over 75 per cent of her body, 21-month-old Emily Woodrow was given only a small chance of survival.

Every inch of her was burned except for her bottom and the soles of her feet. Some parts of her hands were burned to the bone. But Emily defied the odds and clung to life, despite the agonising hourly struggle at the Harborview Medical Center, Seattle, in Washington State, USA.

First, doctors closed her burn wounds using artificial skin, which prevented potentially deadly infection. Every day, twice a day, for six months she underwent rehab to keep her body flexible by stretching her arms and legs.

Eventually the day came when Emily went home, just in time for Christmas.

A chance meeting on a plane saved the life of a transplant patient. If Janet Larson hadn't got the last plane seat next to Allen Van Meader, her sister wouldn't have received the new liver she needed for survival.

Janet was on her way to a New Orleans hospital to donate a kidney to her sick sister, Deborah White. The organ would have bought Deborah crucial time until a liver could be found.

All the flights were full, but Janet managed to get the only seat available, next to Allen. She told him where she was going and he told her he was flying to see his 25-year-old nephew in Kentucky who was dying from an accidental gunshot injury. He had persuaded his sister to donate the young man's organs.

Then he said, 'How about using my nephew's liver for your sister?' They immediately called the hospital to ask if it was possible and discovered that Deborah's blood type did match the boy's.

Even though he was taller and heavier than Deborah, the doctors thought the liver would be suitable.

But a nurse told them it was too late because the boy's organs were being removed as they spoke. Allen begged her to do something quickly, so she ran down the corridor and stopped the procedure.

Just when it was all systems go, the commercial airline scheduled to transport the organ refused to wait 15 minutes for it to arrive. All seemed lost, but their prayers were suddenly answered when an anonymous donor appeared and chartered a jet plane. The liver proved to be a perfect match and the transplant was a complete success.

'My life was saved by a miracle,' said Deborah.

The devotion of a Kansas housewife is proof that love alone can perform miracles. Her husband, Lonny, was diagnosed with manic depression and for 11 years was in and out of psychiatric institutions. Then he stopped taking his medication because he felt better but, without warning, he fell into a vegetative state.

Doctors warned his wife, Roxanna, that he would never recover and advised her to put him in a home permanently. Roxanna, mother of nine children, had worked in nursing homes and knew the importance of keeping patients moving to avoid deterioration. With unflinching courage, she resolved to overcome Lonny's catatonic state by carrying him on her back.

She tied his feet to the outside of her own, putting his arms over her shoulders and tying his hands to a belt around her waist. Roxanna pursued this punishing regime for six hours a day, for five years, talking and singing to Lonny to stimulate his brain. She carried her burden as she did her housework and did exercises with him in the hope of reawakening his dormant responses.

After 18 months, she noticed that Lonny's feet were beginning to move independently. Six months after that, Lonny spoke for the first time and at the end of the five years he was able to walk and talk again.

Lonny went on to serve on the board of the hospital where he was once a patient, but he has no memory of the years he lost.

Julie Mills had just 20 minutes to live. A rare virus had attacked her heart and it was rapidly failing. Surgeon Stephen Westaby figured Julie had nothing to lose, so he connected her to a revolutionary artificial heart in the hope of keeping her alive long enough for her own heart to recover.

The pump had been tried three times before in America and each time the patient had died. But this time Julie, a student from Reigate in Surrey, England, survived and became the first person to be saved with the pioneering operation.

The 'heart' beat for her for six days and was then removed. Within a month, she was home and healthy.

Seeing her baby for the first time meant far more to Deborah Catlyn than it does for most mums.

When she conceived her youngest child, Deborah was blind from an acid attack in a nightclub and thought she would never know what her new baby looked like. Eight earlier operations had failed and she had been told she'd never see again.

But four months into her pregnancy, she was given pioneering stem-cell surgery at Queen Victoria Hospital, East Grinstead, Sussex, which 18 months later restored her sight.

When nurses removed the bandages, Deborah saw how much her two sons, Javies, 17, and Beyonta, 11, had grown in two and a half years. Then she picked up toddler Miracle, whom she had never seen, and wept with joy.

When 15-year-old Jeanna Giese was diagnosed with advanced rabies, there was little hope of saving her, as no one had survived the disease without vaccination.

More than a month earlier, a bat that she'd picked up in church and carried outside had bitten her. She'd washed the tiny wound and thought no more about it until she began to have double vision, fatigue, nausea and numbness.

It was another six days before rabies was diagnosed at the Children's Hospital of Wisconsin in Milwaukee, USA, by which time Jeanna's condition had worsened. People bitten by a rabid animal are usually cured with the rabies vaccine if they receive it immediately. If untreated, patients die within days of the symptoms appearing.

Doctors decided to induce a coma with drugs in order to slow down Jeanna's brain activity and give her immune system time to eradicate the virus. A week later, she was brought out of the coma; she gradually regained consciousness and the use of her body.

Jeanna left hospital after ten weeks but faced a long road to full recovery. She had made history as the only person to survive rabies without receiving the vaccine.

Some years ago, the California Institute of Neotic Sciences (the potential and power of consciousness) published hundreds of case reports from worldwide medical journals detailing medical miracles.

One of these described the case of a 51-year-old patient with a fist-sized abdominal tumour that had spread to the liver – a fast-growing and invariably fatal condition. An operation was scheduled, but, when surgeons saw the extent of the cancer, they could only close him up and send him home to die. Twelve years later, the patient walked into the emergency room of a hospital in Boston, Massachusetts, with an infected gall bladder.

The junior surgical resident, Dr Steven Rosenberg, eyed the grizzled old man with barely concealed distaste and dismissed the man's story – of having had terminal cancer that had simply disappeared – as the rambling of an old drunk. But when he checked the man's records he discovered it was true. During the gall bladder operation he performed, Rosenberg probed the man's liver for signs of the cancer. There was nothing. He was astounded, knowing that there had only ever been four cases in the world of a spontaneous and complete cure of stomach cancer.

When Belinda Mahony was born, her parents were told their daughter would never walk or talk. She was the victim of a strange and rare chromosomal abnormality, which afflicts just 17 people worldwide. But, when she was 22, Belinda walked confidently on to the stage at Australia's Adelaide Hilton to sing a programme of songs for guests at Variety's Show of Hearts Ball.

Her miraculous transition from silence to songbird has confounded all medical predictions. Parents Damian and Susan, from Queensland, watched in amazement as their mute daughter became obsessed with the movie The Sound of Music, and gradually began using sign language to mimic the songs.

As she progressed in speech and song development, Belinda battled against the odds to cope with frequent epileptic seizures, operations on her legs and severe depression. She went on to make several CDs, one called Try to Smile that was aimed at uplifting victims of world tragedies.

The world's first heart transplant in 1967 was hailed as a miracle of modern medicine and pioneered the way for the transplantation of almost every organ in the body.

The hands behind the hearts were those of Professor Christiaan Barnard, who performed the groundbreaking surgery at Groote Schuur Hospital in Cape Town, South Africa.

His first attempts at heart transplant were between dogs. Then in 1967 he took the heart of a 25-year-old road accident victim and placed it in the chest of 53-year-old Louis Washkansky. The patient died 18 days later but subsequent heart transplants gradually increased patients' lifespan by up to a quarter of a century.

Barnard was a notorious womaniser and won almost as many hearts as he transplanted.

Chenelle Baker reckons she has had more serious medical problems than most young people. She's battled lupus, diabetes, congestive heart failure, kidney failure and a lung disease. Doctors in Florida say she's been near death at least five times.

After being on oxygen 24 hours a day for three years to control a terminal lung condition, Chenelle decided to put her life in God's hands. She ripped out her oxygen tube and vowed never to depend on it again. Ever since then, she's been breathing on her own and her X-rays prove her lungs have almost fully recovered, to the amazement of her doctors.

One moment Julie Hill was a happily married mother with two young sons. The next she was a cripple in a wheelchair.

Her world fell apart when she broke her spine in a car crash and doctors told her she would never walk again. The tragedy nearly drove her husband, Kevin, to suicide as he struggled to look after their sons, aged five and seven.

82

Then Julie was offered the chance to become a guinea pig for electronic implants that might enable her to walk.

'I had nothing to lose,' said the gutsy Portsmouth mum. After a nine-hour operation in Salisbury, Wiltshire, Julie had to wait four long anxious days before the device could be tested.

Incredibly it worked and Julie watched her legs being lifted off the bed as the implants stimulated her nerves. Although walking far was too difficult, Julie persuaded the scientists to adapt the system to enable her to ride a bike. Now the world's first paraplegic 'bionic woman' can join her family on weekend cycling trips.

The day before her 20th birthday, Shelly Roush got up early to prepare for a climbing trip from the summer camp where she was working.

Her job was to stand at the bottom of Annapolis Rock, on the Appalachian Trail in Maryland, USA, and anchor the ropes. But when she stepped off the cliff she realised, too late, that she had grabbed the wrong rope. It was only 20 feet long and the ground was 90 feet below.

She hurtled helplessly into space and crashed on to the stony floor. She ruptured her aorta (the major artery carrying blood away from the heart), broke her upper and lower jaw, both wrists, her left hip, two ribs, shattered her right thighbone, left arm and six front teeth.

The camp had just bought new mobile phones so were able to call for help, but because the area was so inaccessible it took the helicopter and paramedics two hours to reach and rescue her. They tried to insert an intravenous drip into her arm but couldn't find a vein, so they decided to risk an extra 30 minutes to take Shelly to a trauma unit in Baltimore. Here doctors discovered the ruptured aorta and operated for 12 hours to repair it.

Shelly eventually returned to college and graduated, but she believes that several small events added up to make one big miracle possible: she had survived a fall which had killed someone else a year earlier; the camp had just acquired new mobile phones; she was taken to the trauma centre where the ruptured aorta was detected; and, above all, had the medics been able to insert an IV, it would have increased her fluid level and almost certainly killed her.

The survival of a toddler, whose heart stopped beating for two hours when she was found, frozen solid, in the snow, amazed Canadian doctors.

The 18-month-old had wandered out at night and been found curled up four hours later in temperatures of minus 22 degrees Fahrenheit, frozen face down with her toes and fingers iced together. Her mouth was frozen shut, her eyelids miniature icicles and her arms and legs purple with frostbite.

Erika Nordby was rushed to hospital clinically dead, suffering from severe hypothermia with a body temperature of only 60 degrees Fahrenheit – well below the normal temperature.

'When Erika arrived, her heart had stopped

for at least two hours,' said Dr Allan De Caen, of the Stollery Children's Hospital in Edmonton, Alberta. 'By every textbook definition she was dead. But we didn't give up.'

His team warmed Erika's body with a heated blanket and mattress, and prepared to attach her to a heart bypass machine to drain her blood, heat it and pump it back into her body. Suddenly, her heart started beating on its own and her temperature started rising rapidly.

'It was a miracle,' the doctor said. 'Clearly something or someone was on this little girl's side.'

Erika left hospital after five and a half weeks with only tiny scars on her frostbitten toes.

Some miracles take a little longer than others to make an appearance. Gary had been in a coma for more than seven years after being shot in the head, and his family had pretty much given up hope of his making any recovery.

When he developed a fever and lung infection, Gary was transferred from a nursing home to a hospital in Chattanooga, Tennessee. Fluid was removed from his lungs and he was given antibiotics. As his fever broke, something astounding happened. Gary started to mumble.

Then he spoke coherently to his sister, Lisa, and was soon asking questions and telling jokes. When his sons, then 12 and 20, walked into the room, he recognised them instantly, though they'd been seven years younger when he last saw them.

Neurologist Dr Ronald Cranford said this kind of dramatic change in a coma patient was 'phenomenally rare', and Gary's doctor could give no medical explanation for his recovery.

# CHAPTER THREE:
# Births and Babies

# BIRTHS AND BABIES

Thomas Bull wouldn't be alive today without hi-tech medical treatment that saved him from a blood-sucking birthmark. Normally, birthmarks are harmless, but the type Thomas had was extremely rare and affected only five babies a year. Within an hour of his birth, the mark, which stretched across his shoulders and back, started to absorb life-threatening quantities of blood. Doctors at London's Great Ormond Street Hospital gave him blood transfusions but this only made the growth soak up more blood.

'It became a race against time to get the

situation under control,' said dad, David Bull. 'Things looked pretty grim.'

Radiologist Dr Derek Roebuck decided to risk a technique never tried on a patient as young as Thomas, which would block the blood vessels with tiny plastic balls. A catheter was inserted into the baby's groin and fed up to his shoulder. Then the balls were pushed along and into the birthmark where they became wedged into the vessels to stop the flow of blood. Thomas was also given an anti-cancer drug to slow down the reproduction of the birthmark blood cells.

'Without this treatment the outlook would have been extremely poor for Thomas,' said Dr Samira Syed. 'His survival is really a miracle.'

Miracles don't come much smaller than baby Georgina Woods, who measured only six inches at birth. Doctors in Cardiff, Wales, gave no chance of survival to the mite, who weighed in at a mere 12oz when she was born just 22 weeks into her mum Marissa's pregnancy.

'She looked like a drenched mouse,' recalled Marissa. 'Then I heard the faintest squeal and I knew she was alive.'

No one thought she'd make it through the first hour, but Georgina proved the experts wrong, clinging to life minute by minute as her mother waited and willed her to pull through. Marissa was able to hold her baby after four weeks, and took her home when she was four months old. Since then, Georgina has blossomed into a healthy little girl.

When five-month-old Kaylee Davidson was given the ultimate gift of life, she became Britain's first successful baby heart transplant patient.

The viral condition cardiomyopathy was slowly killing Kaylee by destroying her heart muscles when the life-saving operation was performed in 1987 at the Freeman Hospital in Newcastle upon Tyne.

Her mother, Carol, recalls how scary it was to see her tiny daughter face the pioneering surgery, especially since it hadn't been successful before.

'We couldn't give up,' she said. 'This transplant was like a miracle to us.' Kaylee grew into a healthy adult and even represented Great Britain in the World Transplant Games.

Janette Rehua's first baby was placed in her arms and left to die. Born at 24 weeks, the paediatrician had given the tiny infant virtually no chance of survival.

'Your daughter will just close her eyes and go to sleep. Very, very soon,' he told Janette gently. Even if she did live, the child had a clot on her brain and would be brain-damaged, lung-damaged, blind and deaf.

The distraught young mother handed the baby over to a nurse before she could become too attached to her and sat numbly waiting for the news that would break her heart. Her husband, Mark, sat by the baby's crib and prayed. His daughter clung to life against all the odds and three times he and Janette refused to let the doctors switch off her life support.

Four hours later, 'amazing Grace' was not only still alive but breathing by herself. She was transferred to a ventilator and given medical aid, which would have happened sooner if she had arrived a week later. At that time in New Zealand, where she was born, the law decreed that babies were viable only at 25 weeks and beyond.

Fourteen weeks later, Janette and Mark were able to take Grace, weighing 5lb, home for Christmas. Grace thrived and grew into a normal healthy teenager, living in Australia.

It's hard to imagine the horror felt by Tami and Thom Whetmore when doctors told them their newborn daughter had no face.

Juliana was born with a rare genetic disorder known as Treacher Collins Syndrome and doctors at Shands Jacksonville Medical Center in Florida, USA, said it was the worst case they had ever seen.

They had to perform immediate plastic surgery to uncover the baby's left eye and open up an airway so she could breathe. She was missing 30 to 40 per cent of the bones in her face. She had no upper jaw, no cheekbones, no eye sockets, no ears and a malformed mouth and nose. A generation ago, Juliana surely would have died. But with the miracles of modern medicine, surgeons are painstakingly reconstructing her face and estimate it will take at least 50 operations.

Every baby is special, but Millie-An Pittman is one in thirteen million! Unknown to mum, Lisa, and the medical staff in Letchworth, Hertfordshire, the baby had developed in her abdomen instead of her womb.

She survived only because the placenta became attached to her bowel, which provided a source of nutrients and oxygen. Despite being scanned throughout the pregnancy, Lisa's rare condition was discovered only when an emergency Caesarean was performed. Millie-An weighed in at a healthy 8lb 7oz, but Lisa lost 12 pints of blood and needed major surgery.

There are only a hundred recorded cases of both mother and child surviving a full-term abdominal pregnancy. Consultant surgeon Douglas Salvesen, who delivered the baby at The Lister Hospital in Stevenage, said, 'I don't like using the word 'miracle' but this baby really is one.'

When Milagros Cerron was born, she was immediately dubbed 'the little mermaid' because her legs were fused together like a fish tail. Usually babies with this defect, known as sirenomelia, die within days of birth but Milagros, who was born to a poor Peruvian family, is a survivor. When she was a year old, a medical team in Lima performed a complex operation to separate the baby's legs. She faces at least 15 years of surgery to correct her condition, including the reconstruction and repair of internal organs, but her doctors hoped she'd be walking by her second birthday.

Milagros, whose name means 'miracles' in Spanish, is only the second patient in the world to have this operation. The first was Tiffany Yorks, now a teenager, who began treatment at the Tampa Shriners Hospital for Children in Florida, USA, when she was just 25 days old. She astounded hospital staff and her family by walking for the first time at the age of three.

The term 'sirenomelia' is believed to derive from the Greek and Roman mythological characters that had the head and upper body of a human and the tail of a fish. The first case was documented in 1542.

Gemma Barrett was devastated when she lost one of the twins she was carrying. Ten weeks later, she miscarried the second. Doctors at St George's Hospital in Tooting, London, performed a standard procedure to clear her womb and Gemma went home to mourn with husband, Angus.

But their grief turned to joy when Gemma returned to see the doctor who discovered another heartbeat. Incredibly, she was still pregnant with a third baby.

In her 24th week Gemma fell, triggering her contractions, but three days later Janaya was born by Caesarean section and weighing 1lb 10oz. The child, who was determined to survive, then faced battles with septicaemia, two bouts of pneumonia and infections. She also had a hole in the heart, which was operated on at Guy's Hospital.

'The doctors said the odds of her living were billions to one,' said Gemma. 'She's a miracle many times over, and a born fighter.'

They called her their mini miracle, the Italian baby girl born in a Florence hospital weighing just 10oz! Stretched out, she measured only ten inches from head to toe, and could sit curled in an adult's hand.

Nicknamed 'Pearl' by the medical team, the infant was delivered during her mother's 27th week of pregnancy.

'We were completely taken aback by her size,' said paediatrician Margarita Psaraki. 'The weight at that stage of development is usually double hers. This was an absolute record.'

Dr Firmino Rubaltelli, who was in charge of the medical team, said the baby's survival was 'a true and proper miracle'.

Special instruments had to be designed to help care for the baby because she was so small, but medics predicted she would have a normal life without medical complications. The parents, who have chosen to remain anonymous, took their daughter home three and a half months later when the baby weighed 4.4lb.

Every day Stephanie Yarber cradles her miracle baby and gives thanks to her twin sister who made the impossible happen.

Melanie made medical history by donating tissue from one of her ovaries during the five-hour operation at St Luke's Hospital in St Louis, Missouri. It was Stephanie's only hope of motherhood after she suffered a premature menopause at just 13, and egg donation from Melanie had failed.

Within months of the procedure, the first in the world, Stephanie discovered she was pregnant and she gave birth to 7lb 15oz Anna Grace in an Alabama hospital.

Born with three potentially fatal heart defects, Isabella Cook wasn't given much hope of living very long. When she was ten days old, doctors in Harrogate, Yorkshire, diagnosed dextra cardia, a condition in which Isabella's heart was on the right side of her chest instead of the left. This prevented it from pumping blood effectively around her body.

Her arteries were the wrong way round and dangerously narrow, and the main artery was attached to only one ventricle instead of both. On top of this, she had a hole in her heart. Any one of the three problems could have killed her, but Isabella became the only British baby to survive these defects.

'We turned pale when the doctor reeled off all the things that were wrong with our little girl,' said mum, Patty. 'It was so hard to take in that we might lose our first baby.'

But Isabella came through two gruelling surgeries before she was strong enough to go home with Patty and her husband, Andrew, who knew that every day their baby lived was another miracle.

In April 1999, Isabella celebrated the day the doctors feared she would never see – her first birthday.

A Mexican woman delivered a healthy baby boy after performing a Caesarean section on herself with a kitchen knife.

The unidentified 40-year-old lived in a rural area without electricity or running water, an eight-hour drive from the nearest hospital. She had lost a baby previously due to complications during labour.

According to Dr R F Valle, of the Dr Manuel Velasco Suarez Hospital in San Pablo, 'She took three glasses of hard liquor and, using a kitchen knife, sliced her abdomen in three attempts. She delivered a male infant who breathed immediately and cried.'

Before losing consciousness, the woman told one of her children to call a local nurse for help. After the wound was stitched with a sewing needle and thread, the mother and baby were taken to hospital.

Brandon Connor's life was blighted before he was born. During routine ultrasound when mum, Kristin, was eight months pregnant, doctors spotted a tumour on the baby's spine.

He was born in Atlanta, Georgia, two days after the 11 September 2001 attacks on New York, and a few weeks later the tumour was diagnosed as neuroblastoma, one of the most aggressive childhood cancers.

His parents faced a terrible dilemma. To operate on it would risk paralysis. To leave it would risk death. Doctors advised them to wait and Brandon was given scans and ultrasound regularly for the next two years.

When the toddler developed a fever and abdominal pains, they feared their borrowed time was over and the surgery was scheduled. But when the last scan was taken before the operation, doctors couldn't believe what they saw. The tumour had disappeared.

'I just can't tell you how we felt,' said Kristin. 'Here it was, the 12th hour. It was a miracle.'

The birth of a baby boy in a Californian hospital gave medical staff more reason to celebrate than most arrivals do.

For three and a half months they had tenderly nursed the infant's brain-dead mother, watching and praying that the foetus would develop sufficiently. At 32 weeks, the 4lb 15oz baby was delivered by Caesarean section and, minutes later, doctors disconnected the ventilator that had been keeping his mother, Trisha Marshall, alive since she was shot in the head during a robbery attempt.

When she had been admitted to Highland Hospital in Oakland and was found to be 17 weeks pregnant, doctors didn't think the baby would survive because they predicted the mother's heart and lungs would fail within two weeks. They hooked her up to a respirator and feeding tube anyway and Trisha defied the odds to produce a healthy son.

Aven the most sceptical admit that Patrick Boaventura's arrival into the world was nothing short of miraculous.

He was born during a road accident in which his mother's body was cut in half. The infant was found lying in snow by the roadside with the umbilical cord still attached to his dead mother, Olga Maria Nunes Bera-Cruz.

Olga was eight months pregnant and travelling in a tractor with the child's father when he lost control on an icy road and hit an embankment in Kentucky, USA. She was thrown clear but hit a sign, which severed her torso. Medics said the baby survived only because the umbilical cord was still attached. When they reached the scene, he was blue and motionless but just breathing after lying in the snow for almost an hour. Paramedics cut the cord and gave the baby oxygen during the 15-minute drive to the hospital.

'I prayed more than I've ever prayed before,' said one paramedic.

Though a continent separates them, Radha Patel is closer to her daughter's children than any grandmother in the world. That's because she was their surrogate mother, carrying the fertilised embryos from her daughter, Lataben Nagla, and giving birth to Neel and Nandini.

'These babies are a miracle,' said Radha, who lives in Gujarat, India. 'They've brought so much joy into our family.'

Radha, who was 46 when she had the babies, went into hiding during the last stages of the pregnancy because she didn't want the stigma of being a surrogate mother to upset her four other children.

The twins now live with Lataben, who is unable to have children of her own, and her husband, Aakash, in Ilford, Essex, England. But they will always be bound in spirit to the woman who gave them life.

Archie Thompson weighed a normal 8lb 4oz at birth. By the age of two, he weighed a colossal six stone! His parents feared for his health as he became breathless and even had a heart attack. They were warned that Archie might not live for more than another year.

Archie is a victim of Momo syndrome, a condition so rare that it's believed only three other people in the world suffer from it. It was first observed by doctors in São Paulo, Brazil, in 1993. Momo stands for macrosomia (excessive birth weight), obesity, macrocephaly (large head) and ocular (eye) abnormalities.

Social services checked that Archie wasn't being overfed at his home in East Sussex and, when the local hospital monitored his eating, they were surprised to find that he ate perfectly normally for his age while continuing to gain weight at an alarming rate.

When Jenny Grove* watches her five-year-old twin daughters playing, she counts her blessings and tries not to imagine the third child who would have made them triplets.

But it's hard for Jenny to forget. While Elena is perfectly healthy, her sister, Lily, was born with some of the third baby's organs inside her. She has two spines, two colons, four kidneys and two uteruses. After 15 operations, including one to

107

fuse the bottom of both her spines together, she has defied doctors' predictions and can walk with assistance. More surgery lies ahead for the Florida youngster.

Jenny viewed Lily's survival as a miracle. Then she began hoping for one of her own as she faced a battle with a recurrence of cancer.

*not her real name

The world's smallest baby tipped the scales at a mere 8.6oz when she was born in Chicago, USA.

Rumaisa Rahman was the twin sister of Hiba, who weighed 1lb 4oz. They were delivered 15 weeks early by Caesarean section at Loyola University Medical Center after doctors became concerned about their development in the womb. Their parents, Shaik and Mohammed, couldn't hold their daughters for two months because the babies were in incubators and on drips.

Despite Rumaisa's size, ultrasounds didn't detect any bleeding in her brain, which is a common complication, and doctors predicted a healthy future for both babies.

The birth of a baby to a 66-year-old Romanian woman shook the world in January 2005. Adriana Iliescu became the oldest recorded mother when she gave birth to a 3lb girl, Eliza Maria, in Bucharest.

Ms Iliescu said she had always wanted to be a mother but had been unable to conceive naturally. After nine years of fertility treatment, she became pregnant with twins, but one died in the womb.

'Eliza was a gift from God,' she said.

Dr Paul Hinkes could find no other word to describe the survival of Amanda Thomas and her newborn son, Charlie. 'This is a miracle baby. A remarkable triumph.'

Amanda, 26, developed viral pneumonia during her pregnancy and was admitted to Providence Holy Cross Medical Center, Los

Angeles, California. Her condition worsened, causing fluid to build up around her heart and lungs, and her kidneys began to fail.

The chances of both mother and baby surviving were slim at best. With her body failing, doctors decided to put Amanda into a drug-induced coma in the hope of stabilising her until the baby could be delivered. That way, maybe one of them would live.

As doctors prepared to perform a Caesarean, Amanda's husband, George, was warned that the procedure could cause her to bleed to death. Then something completely unexpected happened. Amanda's comatose body went into contractions and she gave birth, 15 weeks early, to a 1lb 10oz boy.

Mother and baby were put on life support and, a month later, Amanda awoke from her coma and was able to take little Charlie home.

Jane Ingram made medical history when she gave birth to triplets, one of whom had developed outside her womb.

110

A team of 26 medical staff at King's College Hospital in London delivered the babies in a nerve-racking two-hour operation. The two girls, Olivia and Mary, arrived by Caesarean section, but Ronan had to be cut from a sac that had grown around him.

The case astounded doctors because, if left to grow, most ectopic pregnancies – where the foetus develops in the fallopian tube – cause the tube to rupture, leading to the death of the baby and often the mother.

This was the first case of its kind, but doctors said the miracle baby was unlikely to suffer any effects from his remarkable start to life.

Nailijah Foster cheated death from the day she was born. The miracle baby had two open-heart surgeries and five other operations. She had one lung, no spleen and could breathe only with the help of an oxygen tube.

Then, when she was two, Nailijah defied death yet again when her nurse snatched the child from her pushchair a split second before

111

a woman fleeing police crushed it to pieces with a four-wheel drive.

The nurse, Jean Caseby, was taking the toddler for an outing in Frankford, West Virginia, USA, when the stolen car came out of nowhere and ran into them. Caseby suffered leg injuries but saved the child's life.

A 19-year-old American woman was rushed to hospital in Tacoma, Washington, with a gunshot wound to her head. She didn't make it.

But less than an hour later, her 7lb baby girl was born in Tacoma General Hospital and survived, despite doctors' fears she would suffer organ damage because of oxygen deprivation.

For several days, Jeanene Gordon struggled for survival until she could keep herself alive sucking on a bottle.

D octors were able to save the life of an unborn twin by performing major laser surgery in the womb.

112

Paris and Chelsea White had a rare condition in which they shared one placenta. Chelsea's blood was being carried into Paris's circulation, depriving Chelsea of vital oxygen and nutrients. The only hope was laser surgery, but Chelsea died a day after the operation. Doctors at King's College Hospital, London, gave Paris little chance of making it but she was born a month later, along with her dead sister.

'We had joy and sorrow, but without the laser surgery, we wouldn't have our miracle baby, Paris,' said dad Mark White.

# CHAPTER FOUR:
# Super Miracle Mums

# SUPER MIRACLE MUMS

Supermum Kelly Johnson stunned doctors by giving birth three times in just 16 months.

First came Alanha, followed eight months later by Chloe. Brother Kieron arrived eight months after that. Now the family, from Buckhaven in Fife, Scotland, are aiming for an entry in the Guinness Book of Records for the most individual births in the shortest time.

Jane Croad set a record of her own by giving birth to two babies in nine months – and they're not twins. She went into labour with her first child just 26 weeks into her pregnancy. Elizabeth was born weighing 2lb 10oz, and spent the first eight weeks in a special care unit.

Soon after Jane and her partner, David Protheroe, took the baby home, Jane discovered she was pregnant again. But after only 22 weeks, Jane was rushed into the University Hospital of Wales, Cardiff, where she gave birth to Isabelle. The baby weighed just 1lb 3oz and was given a 5 per cent chance of survival.

She made it, and four months later went home, weighing 5lb, to get to know the sister who is only 36 weeks older than her.

'Most women have a baby at the end of a 40-week pregnancy. I had two in less than that,' said Jane.

A Romanian mother with two wombs gave birth to identical twins – two months apart. Catalin Tescu was born on 11 December. His brother, Valentin, followed 59 days later. It happened after mum Maricica, 33, conceived and the egg fertilised in the fallopian tube

118

and split in two. Each half travelled into a different womb.

Brave mum Natalie Main risked total blindness to have the baby she longed for. But her courage paid off when she gave birth to son, Sean – and, amazingly, regained the sight she'd almost lost to a rare disease.

Natalie, 27, was diagnosed with the incurable condition uveitis, an inflammation of the inner eye that causes 10 per cent of blindness in Britain. Distressing treatments, including chemo-therapy, drugs and laser therapy, could do nothing to halt the advance of her disease, and she was warned that she could lose her vision completely if she had a baby because she would have to stop taking her drugs during pregnancy.

When she discovered she was expecting, Natalie refused to heed the warnings. She battled through her pregnancy hardly able to see anything. She couldn't drive, watch television or read.

An emergency Caesarean was performed

119

when her high blood pressure started to affect her sight, and doctors at Ayrshire Central Hospital in Scotland feared the worst. But, when Sean was born, Natalie realised she could see her precious son and her sight was better than it had been in years.

'It was the most amazing moment of my life,' she said. 'He is my miracle baby.'

Natalie Brown made medical history by becoming the first test-tube baby to give birth to a child of her own.

Natalie, sister of the first-ever test-tube baby Louise, calls her daughter, Casey, her 'double miracle'. The baby was conceived naturally and born healthy despite cynics' fears of abnormalities in second-generation IVF births.

Natalie, who became a mum at 17, was the 40th test-tube baby in Britain. She and Louise took Casey to meet one of the doctors who helped 'create' them, Professor Robert Edwards.

When Louise was born in 1978, she was hailed a miracle of modern science.

# CHAPTER FIVE:
## Wartime

# WARTIME

Ray Holmes will always be remembered as the man who saved Buckingham Palace from destruction by German bombs.

On 15 September 1940, the 26-year-old pilot joined his squadron in the skies over London where enemy aircraft had unleashed 5,000 tons of high explosives that month. A group of Dornier bombers, the pride of the Luftwaffe fleet with their 60-foot wingspan, had been sighted, believed to be en route to the capital.

Ray climbed into his tiny Hurricane fighter, with only a 40-foot wingspan, and ascended to 15,000 feet from where he could see the carnage below in a heavily bombed South London. He noticed with horror that Buckingham Palace had also received two direct hits.

Suddenly the skies all around him were filled with enemy aircraft. Ray attacked, downing one plane and chasing after the other two. One deliberately released a trail of thick, black oil from a flame-thrower in a rear gun emplacement, which coated Ray's windscreen. When the oil cleared, Ray saw that the plane ahead of him was heading straight for the palace. He frantically pressed the button to fire the machine guns in each wing, but neither would work. Now his adrenaline was flowing furiously and his anger and emotion roused to a fever pitch. There was only one thing left to do: he aimed his Hurricane straight at the Dornier's fuselage in a 500mph collision. 'It was just a gut reaction,' he said afterwards.

Bystanders below in Hyde Park watched, horrified, as Ray's plane smashed into the enemy's. The tail broke off the German craft, sending it into a somersault that snapped the wing tips. Then it spiralled downwards as the crew parachuted out. Ray bailed out at 10,000 feet, but as the remains of his plane plummeted to the ground he was hit by his own tail fin, injuring his hand. He managed to get his chute open with his left hand but, as he was landing, the chute got caught on a roof. He ended up suspended with his feet dangling in a water barrel but, miraculously, alive.

Veteran comedian Eric Sykes believes his late mother was the guardian angel who kept him safe throughout World War II.

Apart from saving him from the amorous advances of his gay roommate, she protected him from attack when his unit accidentally strayed almost into no-man's-land and camped for two days without the Germans noticing.

Then, on Christmas Eve 1944, Eric and an air force friend drove on leave from their base in Holland to Brussels. Suddenly, they heard the sound of an enemy aircraft and ducked as the Messerschmitt flew over very low. They knew they were sitting ducks but, instead of shooting them, the pilot waggled his wings and disappeared into the distance.

To this day, Eric has no idea why they weren't killed. If the plane had been out of ammunition, it wouldn't have been flying away from Germany and towards Brussels. The only explanation was that it was one of the many miracles in his life that Eric attributes to his mum, Harriet, who died giving birth to him in 1923.

Amid the horrors of war, acts of kindness mean a great deal. Herman Rosenblatt never forgot the little girl who threw bread and apples to him as he starved in a German concentration camp.

His father had died and his mother had been sent to Treblinka to be gassed. At 12, Herman was orphaned and hungry. One day, he was walking near the camp's barbed-wire fence when he saw a small girl standing there. He asked if she had anything to eat, and she tossed him an apple.

Every day after that, the girl returned with some food, and both children were at risk of being shot by the SS if they were seen. When he was shipped to another camp in 1944, Herman didn't see the girl again. Nine months later, the Allies liberated the camps and Herman was freed on the very day he was scheduled for the gas chamber.

Eventually, he moved to New York. Though engaged three times, he refused to wed because he didn't feel he'd found his soul mate. In 1957, Herman went on a blind date and met Roma, whom he discovered he'd met once before when they were out with a group of friends in Israel. That was remarkable in itself, but when they started talking about their war experiences, they couldn't believe their ears when they put the pieces in place and realised that he was the boy she'd thrown food to in the concentration camp.

'You saved my life and I'm going to marry you,' said Herman impulsively, though they'd only just met. Eleven months later, they fulfilled their destiny and wed.

Nearly 900 men perished in the worst naval disaster in US history when the USS Indianapolis was torpedoed by the Japanese on its way back from delivering the atomic bomb. The 317 survivors were at death's door when they were pulled from shark-infested waters after floating for five days and four nights.

It took only 12 minutes for the 610-foot heavy cruiser to sink after it was hit by two torpedoes. By then, most of the crew had abandoned ship and plunged into the sea between Guam and the Philippines. By day, they burned beneath the merciless sun. Some were covered in oil and were literally fried. By night, they shivered in the cold water, praying for rescue.

Then the sharks came. With their legs dangling in the water beneath their life jackets, the men were easy targets.

'We'd hear a scream, and the water would turn red,' recalls Seaman First Class Cox.

After a couple of days without food or water, the men began to hallucinate. They'd take off their life jackets and 'slip back to the ship for a drink of water' or swim off to an imaginary island, never to be seen again. One by one they died, as the days wore on, until a pilot spotted the oil slick left by the Indianapolis. It took another day to lift the stricken men, many badly burned, from the water. As rescuers grabbed them by their arms, their skin would come clean off. Those who survived it marvel that they did so.

War is a time of heightened emotions, when human resources are challenged to the limit. People who couldn't be close to their loved ones sometimes found other ways to connect with them.

During World War I, the mother of two soldiers who had been posted to France woke in the night and saw a uniformed figure standing at the foot of her bed. The figure pointed a finger to his forehead and said, 'It went through here.'

Later in the war, the family was notified that one brother was a prisoner of the Germans, while the other had been killed. When her son came home after the war, the mother asked what had happened to his brother. He pointed a finger to his forehead and said: 'He was shot through here.'

Corporal George Webber miraculously survived being buried alive and gnawed by rats during World War I.

The Devon-born railway porter was drafted into the First Monmouthshire Regiment and, during the German counter-offensive of 1918, he was injured by shrapnel, then bayoneted by advancing German troops. When his comrades found him unconscious and drenched in blood, they assumed he was dead and buried him in a shallow grave, intending to rebury him later.

Webber came round and heard voices. Horrified, he realised he was lying in his own tomb and he had to get out of there quickly, before he suffocated. He pushed an arm through the soil and hoped someone would realise that he was still alive. By the time he was dug out, his chest had been badly eaten by rats. He returned to active service but inhaled mustard gas, which destroyed the bottom half of his lung.

When the war ended, he was on crutches but still in uniform. Once on Civvy Street he faced new battles, with a string of 23 operations on his battered but indomitable body.

At 9am on 1 September 1945, two American civilian prisoners of war were asked if they could make an American flag in time for the next day's signing of the Japanese surrender. The idea was to raise the flag at Fukuoka Camp No 6 in Orio at the same time as the official ceremony. The men were given 24 hours to complete their task and an armful of red, white and blue parachutes, which had been used by the Americans to drop clothing and food into the camp during the last days of the war.

They used white cement sacks to make patterns for the 96 stars they needed – 48 on each side of the flag – and made glue from rice gruel to stick them on. Rodney Kephart sat up all night using an old Japanese sewing machine to assemble the flag and, when it was finished, fell into bed exhausted. When he was awakened by the sound of a bugle playing the last post, he wept, heartbroken because he had missed the historic raising of the colours that he'd made possible.

The Victory Flag eventually came into the possession of the Idaho Historical Society that, in 1984, lent it for temporary display at two functions. As there was a week's gap between them, Kephart, who happened to be attending the events, was asked to look after the flag. He couldn't believe his luck to be reunited with an emblem that meant so much to him. But he was overwhelmed when officials discovered that Kephart had been its maker and told him he could keep it.

'I felt it was a miracle that the flag I'd made 46 years earlier far away in a Japanese prisoner of war camp had been returned to me,' he said.

Stumbling back to his ship in the blackout, the gunner looked out for the sentry's flashlight to

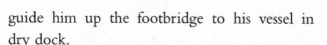
guide him up the footbridge to his vessel in dry dock.

He was suddenly gripped by an inexplicable fear, which froze him to the spot. Trembling all over, he couldn't put one foot in front of the other. When the sentry shone his torch again, Ray could see that he was several feet from the bridge but both feet were literally on the edge of the dry dock – and a 30-foot fall below. Six hours later, as he went on his watch, he was told that a crewmember had been found dead, having fallen into the dry dock where he'd been standing.

Ray cheated death on two other occasions during the war and he believes it was because a guardian angel was watching over him. When he reached Bombay, he asked to be assigned to the same ship as two friends, and the petty officer begrudgingly agreed. The vessel Ray was originally meant to join blew up, killing more than 5,000 people.

While in the East End of London, he waited for a bus to go from the Bakers Arms in Leyton to Clapton, via Lea Bridge Road. When the bus didn't turn up, he decided to walk. Just as he arrived, he heard an explosion and discovered that a V2 rocket had fallen on Lea Bridge Road station, wrecking a bus that had stopped outside – Ray's bus.

When Rommel ordered a retreat after the battle of El Alamein in October 1942, Private Lionel Watson was relieved. But the worst time of his life was yet to come. On the day of the retreat, his tank came under fire and Private Watson was left for dead inside the blazing vehicle, surrounded by the bodies of his colleagues.

When he regained consciousness, he managed to pull his trapped hand away from the searing metal, but lost all the fingers on his left hand. Lying on the ground, bleeding and badly injured, Private Watson was found by medical staff and put on a stretcher. But as they carried him to an ambulance they, too, were machine-gunned and died in a hail of bullets.

Once again, Private Watson miraculously

survived, despite receiving a bullet through his chin. No one knows how the stricken soldier crawled the long distance back to allied lines, but he made it and was taken to hospital in Cairo where he remained unconscious for four months. He was so severely burned that his ears, scalp and half his fingers were missing, and then he caught malaria.

When Private Watson was returned to England, he was taken to a hospital in Basingstoke where he was treated by pioneering surgeon Sir Archie McIndoe. As one of McIndoe's guinea pigs, Private Watson had 37 skin-graft operations.

Two hundred people crowded into a public bomb shelter in Tel Aviv, huddled together and praying as they awaited the imminent missile attack. When it came, the shelter took a direct hit – 550lb of explosives – that brought the world crashing down around them.

An acrid smell of burning sulphur filled their nostrils and they choked on the thick cloud of black dust that filled the room. Some bodies were thrown into the air. Others had thrown themselves on to the ground and were screaming wildly. But, when the noise stopped and the dust began to clear, people got to their feet and looked round in silent amazement. Not one single soul had been injured or killed.

The next morning, Prime Minister Yitzhak Shamir visited the area with the Mayor of Tel Aviv. Shamir was shocked by the damage he saw and asked Mayor Lahot if anyone had been in the shelter at the time of the attack.

He replied that there had been, and all 200 were saved by a miracle.

After World War I, the miracle of Christmas always had special resonance for the men of the Berkshire Regiment.

On the night of 23 December 1914, they were lying war-weary in their trenches, savouring a rare peace in their sector of the front line. Someone noticed a small sparkling, conical shape above the German parapet

136

opposite. Another followed, and then another, until a whole row twinkled across the inky void of no-man's-land.

Spurred more by curiosity than courage, the British soldiers slowly emerged from their dugouts. At the same time, the German infantrymen rose and approached the Berkshires until they stood face to face amid the barbed wire and shell-craters.

The Germans explained that the tiny trees had been sent so that their troops could continue the cherished custom of lighting them for Christmas. British and German officers met and agreed to hold an informal truce for Christmas Eve and Christmas Day and similar impromptu ceasefires broke out among regiments along the whole length of the Western Front.

Carols and songs in German and English filled the starry night as an unprecedented camaraderie developed between enemies who had been killing each other the day before. As light dawned the next morning on a section near Lille, the sight of no-man's-land still littered with bodies cast a pall on the festive spirit. In a tacit agreement, both sides retrieved the fallen and a joint mass burial service was held, with prayers and readings in both languages.

Now they could celebrate Christmas with the exchange of simple gifts and pooling of food supplies for the festive feasts. Games of football were held using empty bully beef tins as balls; souvenirs, such as uniform buttons and belts, were bartered and, for the lucky few, champagne was drunk.

By Boxing Day, the most amazing truce in military history was over but, for those who survived the war, it was a miracle never to be forgotten.

Every morning, Rabbi Samuel Shapira walked through the Polish village of Prochnik, greeting everyone he met. One of those he saw regularly was a peasant farmer, Herr Mueller, who ignored him at first as relations between Jews and gentiles weren't good. Eventually, though, Mueller warmed to the genial Rabbi and returned the hearty hello.

When the Nazis came, all the Jewish residents in the village were shipped to a concentration camp. Shapira was sent to Auschwitz. As he stood in the selection line, he could see the camp commandant's baton swing left, then right, and he knew that left signified a death sentence, but right meant possible survival.

His heart was racing with fear as he approached the man who would decide his fate. Stiffening with dignity, he lifted his eyes to look at the commandant and their eyes locked.

'Good morning, Herr Mueller,' said Shapira quietly.

'Good morning, Herr Shapira,' replied the other man without perceptible emotion, but swinging his baton to the right.

During the Vietnam War, Rick volunteered for a second tour with the 101st Airborne. He was a door gunner on a night operation when the fuse on one of the flares on board started to burn, filling the chopper with smoke. Rick stumbled and grabbed on to a post as he fell out of the door and ended up suspended from the plane. He knew there were only seconds before the flare detonated, turning the chopper into a fireball.

He faced an agonising dilemma: hang on and be burned to death when the flare exploded, or drop 1,500 feet to his death.

Rick decided to let go and trust that a higher power would save him. Then a miraculous thing happened. Rick found himself back on board the chopper, pushing the flare out of the door. He has no idea how he got there. His crew chief looked at him, shocked.

'He had written me off as dead,' said Rick.

One of the best-known miraculous encounters during World War I occurred during the Battle of Mons.

In August 1914, British and French troops were retreating from a German assault, wearily resigned to their defeat. It seemed that nothing could save them from the enemy's onslaught and they were too exhausted to care. Turning round to check how close the Germans were, they saw instead what they could only describe as 'angels on horseback' riding between them and the enemy. The vision gave them new strength to march on, which undoubtedly saved many lives.

As the wounded soldiers were taken to field hospitals, one after another told the nurses of seeing the angels on the field and the nurses reported a startling serenity in the dying men, as though they had nothing to fear.

Sceptics dismissed these reports as the hallucinations of exhausted men, but then word got back that German soldiers had had similar experiences. They said they found themselves 'absolutely powerless to proceed – and their horses turned around sharply and fled'.

Despite exhaustive research into the incident by experts after the war, no one really knows exactly what happened that day. One fact remains: something miraculous did happen during a crucial stage in the battle and the British Army was preserved from total destruction.

When a Nazi officer discovered Wladislaw Szpilman hiding in the crumbling ruins of Warsaw, the young Jewish musician was starving, freezing cold and near death.

He'd somehow survived alone in the ruined wasteland of the war-torn city, hiding in the warren of ghetto streets. With only ragged clothes to protect him from the harsh winter, he'd existed on water melted from snow by the heat of his body and scavenging for what little food was left.

Now he'd been discovered and it seemed the five-year struggle for survival had been in vain. He waited for the German bullet to slay him but, instead, the officer spoke to him, asking what he did for a living. When Szpilman replied that he was a pianist, Captain Wilm Hosenfeld ordered him to sit down at an ancient piano and play. Though a professional musician before the war, he hadn't touched a keyboard for three years. But now he was playing for his life.

As the strains of Chopin faded, the men heard gunfire as more Germans arrived. Incredibly, the

German officer offered to protect the Jewish musician from his own soldiers, and even brought him food to his attic hiding place until the Russians arrived.

The story of Szpilman's miraculous survival became the theme of the award-winning film The Pianist. Despite his compassion, Hosenfeld was imprisoned and tortured by the Russians and died in captivity, a broken man.

Music also saved the life of concentration camp survivor Shony Alex Braun.

One day an SS officer came into his barracks with a violin and announced that anyone who could play the instrument for the commandant would be given food. Braun and two other desperately hungry prisoners volunteered and were marched away to the commandant's office. The oldest man trembled as he tuned the violin and then coaxed a beautiful sonata from its strings.

'Awful,' screamed the German officer, ordering the guards to beat the prisoner to death with iron bars as the others watched. The second man was so terrified he couldn't play a single note and he, too, was beaten to death. Braun tried to run away but he was pulled back and given the violin.

'I'd never even held an adult-sized violin because I had only played as a small child,' recalled US-based Braun more than half a century after the event. His mind froze as he tried to press his fingers on to the strings. Suddenly, he felt a powerful force seize control of his hands. To his utter amazement, melodic music began to pour from the violin and he recognised the Blue Danube waltz, a tune he'd never played before.

'I knew that God had sent an angel to guide my hands,' he said. Braun was given not only some much-needed food, but also his life.

A soldier on a bomb-clearing mission in Malta in 1941 recalls how his Wing Commander suddenly shouted a word of warning. Instinctively, the search party ran for what little cover there was on the exposed landing area.

Seconds later, a buried bomb exploded. Not one soldier was killed or injured and the officer told them later that he had no idea what had made him call out and save them all from certain death.

In August 1942, 17,000 Jews were crammed into Poland's Lutsk ghetto, where they struggled for survival. When a Ukrainian peasant offered to help Fania Paszi and her family to escape and hide in the town, she agreed to test the escape route first, tearing off the yellow Star of David which denoted her Judaism, and covering her head with a shawl. Her disguise enabled her to slip past the German soldiers and Ukrainian police unchallenged.

The plan was to return the next day and smuggle her entire family out of the ghetto, but, when she approached that morning, a Ukrainian policeman, taking her for a fellow Christian and not a Jew, warned her to stay away as the area had been sealed off for official reasons.

Over the course of the next two days, all the

Jews were led from the ghetto to the outskirts of the city where they were thrown into pits and machine-gunned to death. Fania's courageous expedition had saved her life, but she had lost everyone and everything. Dazed and grief-stricken, she returned to her guide's home and hid in the chimney flue of an outside oven for several months until the Ukrainian, fearing for his own safety, eventually threw her out.

Fania wandered the freezing streets in her tattered cotton dress, hungry, homeless and despairing. On Christmas Eve, she arrived at the manor house of the country warden where she was set upon by the guard dogs, which bit her and ripped her dress. When the warden emerged, Fania begged him to shoot her so she could share the fate of her family. Instead, the warden took her inside into the warm, fed her Christmas Eve dinner and gave her new clothes and a bed for the night.

When the war was over, Fania never forgot the miracle of how the Christian celebration of Christmas saved the life of a Jewess.

The dead and dying outnumbered the survivors at the end of a particularly brutal battle. A stretcher bearing the lifeless body of 24-year-old Jack Traynor was about to be loaded on the mortuary cart when a doctor noticed that the young soldier was still alive.

Despite being hit in the head by shrapnel, which had penetrated his brain, Traynor survived surgery and returned to active service in France ten months later. In August 1915, Traynor crawled from his trench on his elbows and knees across a battlefield to rescue the body of a major. As he reached the man, a burst of machine-gun fire riddled Traynor with bullets and he lay helpless in his own blood until a night patrol could pick him up.

Two bullets had ploughed through his chest, grazing the heart and piercing the lung, while a third had gone through the shoulder, ripping the delicate nerve centre which controls the movement of the arm. The surgeon saved his life a second time, but three further operations failed to repair the damaged nerves in his arm, which was slowly paralysing.

Even when he developed severe epilepsy, for which there was no effective treatment in 1915, Traynor refused to give up hope that he would recover.

Four years after the war ended, he was a physical wreck, skeletal and constantly convulsed. He agreed to an operation on a part of his brain which might be causing the fits, but it not only failed to stop them, but also left him with a gaping hole in his skull.

Just before he was due to be admitted to a hospital for incurables, Traynor joined a pilgrimage to Lourdes. The dying man was lowered into the baths there and returned to the hospice immediately, as attendants feared he might have an epileptic fit. The next day, to the incredulity of all who had seen him before, Traynor got out of bed and washed and shaved himself.

'All those with whom I offered to shake hands started back as though they had seen a ghost,' he recalled.

The three surgeons who had operated on him agreed his arm had been completely restored

148

and the wound to his skull had healed. Few doubted they had witnessed a miraculous cure.

Robert Adkins cradled his friend's injured body in his lap and used his handkerchief to try and stem the flow of blood from a gaping head wound.

Roy Stump had been with a group of soldiers attempting to defuse a mine in Holland when it had blown up, showering him with shrapnel. Adkins, watching a medic remove his best buddy's identity tags, grieved for his loss, but there was a war on and duty called.

Fifty-two years later, Robert got into conversation with a man in a hospital waiting room in Ohio, USA, and, when the subject got round to the war, they discovered they had been in the same battalion. When Robert mentioned his friend's tragic death, the man smiled.

'I'm Roy Stump and I didn't die,' he told an astonished Robert. He explained that he had been critically injured but his life had been saved by an emergency operation in a field tent. He had been transferred to a hospital in Belgium where he had remained for 18 months, recovering from 42 wounds, including one that left him with a metal plate in his head.

Even more amazing was that both men had moved to Lorain, Ohio, USA, after the war and for more than 40 years had been living only a few miles apart.

# CHAPTER SIX:
# Amazing Animals

# AMAZING ANIMALS

It looked like time had run out for the homeless dog sentenced to death at the city pound for being 'too aggressive'.

The one-year-old Basenji mix was herded into the gas chamber in St Louis, Missouri, with dozens of other unwanted dogs, and left to die. But, when animal control supervisor Rosemary Ficken opened the door to remove the bodies 30 minutes later, one dog stood unsteadily among the corpses but with his tail gallantly wagging, very much alive. She telephoned an animal rescuer and begged him to take the dog because she didn't have the heart to gas the feisty mutt again.

The story of the dog's miracle survival touched the hearts of American dog lovers and 700 of them asked to adopt Quentin – named after California's State Prison. He became a symbol of hope for all strays in a national campaign launched to educate the public about animal shelters.

It seemed that nothing could put a smile on the face of little Katie Phillips. Left severely brain-damaged by an evil child-killer, her parents had to accept that their baby would never walk or talk.

Their grief was doubled by the murder of Katie's two-month-old twin sister, Becky, at the hands of Beverly Allitt, the nurse they had trusted and who had almost killed Katie, too.

In 1993, Allitt was convicted of murdering four children and maiming six while in her care at Grantham Hospital, Lincolnshire. She had tried to kill Katie four times by injecting drugs or suffocating her and, at one point, the baby stopped breathing for 42 minutes and was clinically dead.

When Katie was a year old, doctors assessed the long-term damage she had suffered and broke the devastating news to Sue and Peter that their daughter would be a 'vegetable'. At two and a half years old she was like a newborn baby, unable to crawl, sit up or eat solid food. In desperation, her parents raised the money to take Katie to the Dolphin-Human Therapy Center in Key Largo, Florida, USA.

At the end of the first week working with the dolphins, Katie put her feet on the ground and tried to stand up. After regular visits, she learned to walk unaided, to read and to write.

'Since Katie first swam with dolphins, I have begun to believe in miracles,' said Sue.

When six-month old Kyle had a stomach upset, his owner thought the dog must have eaten something unpleasant. He had – a 15-inch bread knife! Vets at the People's Dispensary for

Sick Animals in Leeds don't know how 18-inch-long Kyle survived his unusual meal.

'The knife could have cut his internal organs to shreds at any time,' said a dumbfounded Dr Ann Draper, senior veterinary officer.

Eva Oliver said she had no idea how her Staffordshire bull terrier-collie cross swallowed the serrated knife, but thought it was a miracle he had survived.

Scientists remain confounded by some pets' ability to travel thousands of miles when lost.

• Fido the dog spent two years travelling 990 miles to track down his owner, Lise Deremier, even though she had moved from Mons in Belgium to Gijon in northern Spain.

• An Australian fox terrier called Whisky journeyed 1,860 miles from Darwin to Melbourne in order to get home.

• In 1995, a border collie called Blake was abducted when thieves stole his master's car. It was abandoned in Downham Market, Norfolk, England. Blake took five days to travel 50 miles to

Letheringsett, a mile from his home, where villagers who found his identity disc contacted his owner.

• Linda Thompson and her cat, Sam, moved from Beaver Dam, Wisconsin, USA, to Tucson, Arizona. A year later, Linda moved back to Beaver Dam, but to a different house. She left Sam with a new family in Tucson. Four years later, Linda went to visit the people who had bought her first home in the town and couldn't believe her eyes when she found Sam living there! Somehow, he'd found his way back to his former home – an astounding 1,500-mile journey.

• A cat named Minosch made a similar odyssey after he was lost during a family holiday in Turkey. He turned up 61 days later at their home on the island of Sylt in northern Germany.

• In the ultimate incredible journey, Cheyenne the cat travelled 3,000 miles over seven years before she was reunited with her owner. Pamela Edwards last saw her pet in the garden of her Florida home. Then it vanished. Seven years later, the cat was found strolling along a street in San Francisco, California. Cheyenne was taken to an animal shelter where a scan revealed a microchip, which identified her and her owner. US television personality Ellen DeGeneres flew Pam to California for an emotional reunion with the cat she never thought she'd see again.

'It was incredible, like being reunited with a lost family member after so many years,' she said. 'No one has any idea how Cheyenne travelled so far.'

When Libby the German shepherd seemed to be feeling a bit under par, her owner took her to the vet. He didn't even need to give her an X-ray; he could hear dozens of golf balls rattling around in her stomach.

Libby had swallowed 28 balls during her daily walks around Didsbury Golf Club, Manchester. The vet removed 6lb of balls, gave Libby 30 stitches and suggested she chased birdies instead.

Ray and Carol Steiner couldn't understand why they were sleeping so much. Although Ray was recuperating from a triple bypass operation, and Carol was recovering from foot surgery, they were spending nearly 19 hours a day in bed.

It was a hot summer in Bowling Green, Ohio, USA, and their windows were closed tight because the air-conditioning was going full blast. They felt tired all the time, had headaches, high blood pressure and memory lapses, which the doctor attributed to post-operative fatigue.

The family cat was named Ringo because, instead of meowing when he wanted to go out, he'd drum his paws on the door. One day Carol heard a loud bang on the front door and, when she went to investigate, Ringo was there, apparently having thrown himself at the door. But, when Carol opened the door to let him out, he wouldn't go. She shut the door and returned to bed, but no sooner had she got her leg comfortable than Ringo hurled himself at the door again.

Back Carol hobbled on her crutches to open the door, but still the cat wouldn't go outside. When she opened the door wider, he took a couple of steps and, for the first time in

159

his life, meowed. Every time Carol walked towards him, he meowed again and moved further into the garden, until he had led her all round the house.

Then he started digging into the gravel, though the rough stones made his paws bleed. Eventually Carol moved closer and bent down. Shocked, she realised there was a strong smell of gas coming from the ground. The gas-company serviceman came and tested the meter but assured her there was no leak, so she took him to where Ringo had been digging.

The reading shot off the meter and set off an alarm. It turned out that the leak was so large, the slightest exposure to a spark would have blown up the Steiner house and seven others linked to the system. Methane had been leaking from a crack in the gas main and accumulating in the Steiners' unventilated house. They were suffering from methane poisoning, which was slowly killing them.

Ringo saved more than 20 lives that day and was given an award from the American Humane Association.

It sounds like a shaggy dog story at best, but Henri, a 13-year-old toy poodle, has the scars to prove his near-death experience when he was carried away by a pack of coyotes.

Owner John Turner said he was jogging in the recreation area of a Colorado park one morning when he saw half a dozen coyotes attack the poodle and drag him off to what seemed a certain death. But the next afternoon his wife, Susan, arrived home three miles from the park and found Henri on the doorstep, bloodied but unbowed.

'We were absolutely amazed he was able to get away and that he found his way home because he was really chewed up,' she said.

The Turners raced to the animal clinic where Henri, who weighs only 13lb 8oz, underwent three-hour surgery and emerged with 40 stitches and nine tubes sticking out of him to drain toxins.

'He thinks he's a big dog,' said John. 'He's got real attitude.'

Animals have played a huge role during wartime – eight million horses lost their lives in World War I alone. Here are some of the stories of heroism, sacrifice and courage, which distinguish their behaviour from the ordinary to the miraculous:

• Corporal Jimmy Muldoon's boat had been picked out by a searchlight and was being bombarded by Germany artillery. Suddenly, the craft capsized, pitching the crew into the icy water. Rifleman Khan swam to the shore and started looking around for Jimmy, who couldn't swim. Somehow, through the roar of battle, Khan heard Jimmy's cries for help as he struggled to stop his heavy equipment dragging him under water.

Fortunately, Khan was no ordinary foot soldier. He was an Alsatian, which had been lent for active service by his owners in Surrey and been a star pupil at War Dog Training School. In the summer of 1942, Jimmy became his handler and, two years later, they were despatched aboard an assault craft to take part in the Allied attack on the Dutch island of

Walcheren, a vital obstacle in the advance of the Germans.

Now Khan made a desperate bid to save his master from drowning. Ignoring the falling shells, he plunged back into the sea and swam back and forth in the darkness until he finally found Jimmy, who was on the point of exhaustion. Minutes later and he would have succumbed to the chilly depths. Khan grabbed the collar of his tunic between his teeth and Jimmy clung on to the dog's fur until they reached firm land. Khan was awarded the Dickin Medal, the animal Victoria Cross, for his act of gallantry and loyalty.

• Rob the dog was the most decorated canine in history, winning six ribbons and two military medals. He joined the SAS in 1942 and was frequently parachuted behind enemy lines to round up troops and lead them to safety, barking warnings whenever he sensed the enemy approaching.

• During World War I, dogs were used as messengers. They were lighter and faster than men, and less of an enemy target. A request for ammunition or other vital information was written on a piece of paper and put in a pouch attached to the dog's collar.

One of the most heroic messenger dogs was Satan, a half-breed black greyhound, which helped to save a vital position at Verdun. His handler, a French soldier named Duvalle, saw the dog streaking towards him from enemy lines. But then the dog buckled and crashed to the ground, struck by a bullet. Duvalle stood up on the trench wall in full view of the enemy and shouted, 'Courage, Satan, mon ami. Do it for France!'

Duvalle was mown down in a hail of bullets but Satan, hearing his master's voice, and with his shattered leg hanging uselessly, limped the last few hundred yards to safety. He was bringing a message to the town to hang on because help was at hand. On his back were pouches containing two terrified carrier pigeons, which were dispatched with crucial information for the French artillery.

• During a 1945 Japanese attack against US troops in the Philippines, Bruce didn't wait for his master's command to act. He knew there wasn't a second to hesitate, so the courageous Alsatian hurled himself at three enemy soldiers with fixed bayonets who were poised to finish off two wounded GIs huddling in a foxhole. His action saved not only their lives but also those of others in the unit.

• Twenty years later during the Vietnam War, another dog, named Nemo, despite having been shot in the head, leaped at two Vietcong, knocking them over, which gave US soldiers time to radio for backup. When his handler was shot, the suffering Nemo crawled to the soldier and covered him with his body until help arrived.

• Faith, a tabby cat owned by the vicar of St Augustine's Church in Central London, normally slept upstairs in the vicarage. But on 6 September 1940, she became restless and suddenly lifted her kitten out of its basket and carried it three floors downstairs, where she put it in a wall recess.

Four times the vicar tried to take the kitten upstairs, and each time Faith brought it back. Eventually, the vicar left her alone. Three days later, the house was bombed and crashed in flames around the clever cat and her kitten, which were safe and snug in their recess.

The unspoken communication between animals and humans can be miraculous. Josh, a ten-year-old Down's syndrome boy from Casaville, Missouri, USA, wandered away from his remote country home one freezing winter's night.

Search parties spent 72 hours scouring the woodlands and hills but failed to find Josh. Oscar Neil, one of the searchers, had got lost and was trying to find his way back to the others. He felt his horse quicken her step and, with ears pricked up, set off determinedly up the mountain, away from the direction in which Oscar was wanting to head.

After a mile or so, Oscar could hear the sounds of dogs barking fiercely. Then two wild dogs came charging towards him, growling ferociously. Just beyond them, Oscar could see Josh lying down and the larger dog was barking as if to warn Oscar not to hurt the boy.

Oscar moved gingerly towards them, braced for attack, but the animals allowed him to pick up the semi-conscious Josh and take him to safety on horseback.

He was treated for frostbite but was otherwise unscathed. Oscar believes Josh's miraculous survival was thanks to the protection of the wild dogs, which had kept him warm by lying close to him.

Endal the Labrador not only saved his master's life but also his marriage. Gulf War veteran Allen Parton described himself as 'a lost man' until he met the dog. He had become bitter and depressed after a road accident during the conflict had left him paralysed and without a memory.

The Royal Navy chief petty officer spent three years in hospital, unable to walk, talk or recognise his family. He couldn't remember Sandra, the wife he'd married 19 years earlier. Nor did he have any recollection of his two children.

'My wife and I were close to splitting up,' he said. 'But Endal brought me back to my family.'

The dog learned how to help with daily tasks; when Allen touched his face, Endal fetched his razor. He was also trained to cover his master with a blanket when he suffered from the occasional blackout. When Allen was knocked unconscious by a car outside a Birmingham hotel, Endal covered his master with a blanket, pushed a mobile phone towards his face and alerted hotel staff.

Endal, naturally, was best man when Allen and Sandra decided to renew their marriage vows in Liphook, Hampshire.

The vet did a double take when he saw the bone Poppy the puppy had swallowed – it was more than half her length!

The five-month-old 14-inch-long Lhasa Apso snatched the eight-inch rib from her owners' barbeque table and wolfed it down in one go. It was bigger than any bone in her body and ran the full length of her stomach.

Emergency surgery was needed to save her life.

'We were amazed when we saw it,' said veterinary nurse Natalie Morgan. 'Poppy is a very lucky puppy. She really had a miracle escape.'

Dogs are notoriously loyal to their owners and will risk life and limb if the need arises. But the heroic hound who rescued teenager Lisa Nibley from a fast-flowing river in Oregon, USA, was a perfect stranger. And even more remarkable was the fact that Norman, a yellow Labrador, was totally blind.

He was walking along the riverbank with his owners when they heard screams. Immediately Norman took off, ignoring his master's calls, and plunged into the river where Lisa was drowning.

The girl held on to Norman's tail as he swam back to shore.

During the disastrous floods in southern California in the spring of 1992, an unlikely hero emerged. Weela, a feisty pit-bull terrier, became a superheroine credited with saving the lives of 30 people, 29 dogs, 13 horses and a cat.

Her courageous feats included:

• wading across a swollen river 15 times carrying a 50lb backpack of food to stranded dogs;

• leading a human rescue team safely around quicksand and treacherous holes hidden beneath the water's surface to an island where horses were starving;

• pulling people out of waist-level mud although she weighs only 65lb;

• standing resolutely in front of a group of men, women and children to prevent them from crossing a river at a point where the concealed and deadly undertow would have swept them to their deaths.

'Weela was incredible,' said her proud owners, Lori and Daniel Watkins. 'She just knew what to do to help. When rescuers didn't know how to get across the raging floodwater, Weela located safe routes for them. She was absolutely tireless.'

170

Weela's heroism was recognised with the National Dog of the Year Award.

Jeff Best was not pleased when his wife, Nancy, brought home a Labrador puppy. But he was soon won over by the cute ball of golden fluff and Mia became one of the family in Garberville, Northern California.

As a mum of three, with a busy coffee shop to run, Nancy wasn't surprised when she started feeling tired during the day. She and Mia used to lie on the couch for an afternoon nap. Then Mia developed the habit of sniffing Nancy's clothes and licking the same spot. Nancy thought the dog could detect food from the café.

One afternoon, Mia came bounding in and jumped up at Nancy, nuzzling into the same area on her chest. It was then that Nancy felt the lump. Her doctor, Mark Phelps, diagnosed a virulent form of cancer, which could only be stopped if it was caught early. Surgeons removed 26 lymph nodes from Nancy's armpit but gave her a positive prognosis.

'What Mia did was just remarkable,' said Dr Phelps.

Jeff added, 'The miracle here was Mia's determination to let Nancy know there was something wrong.'

Honey the cocker spaniel got a very different kind of ducking from the one she had expected when she leaped off her owner's boat to check out some quacking.

George Wrigley, who wasn't wearing a life jacket, leaned over to try and haul the dog back on board but ended up joining her in the bitterly cold waters of the Dart estuary in Devon. He struggled in the darkness against the strong current, wind and rain in a vain attempt to reach the marina. For the next hour and a half, George, 55, clung to Honey in conditions it's doubtful he would have survived alone for 20 minutes.

By the time his cries, and Honey's barks, were heard, George was semi-conscious and suffering from hypothermia. Rescuers said he made it only because Honey was with him.

If Sheba the spaniel could talk, she'd dine out for years on the story of how she survived a fall from the notorious clifftop suicide spot Beachy Head.

She was walking with her owner, Tim Castle, and his two sons along the East Sussex beauty spot when Tim took off her lead. Sheba bounded off and then disappeared over the edge of the cliff. It was a sheer drop of 300 feet and Tim didn't even dare look down for the body. He called the local lifeboat crew who happened to be on a training exercise close by. They rushed to the scene and couldn't believe their eyes. There was Sheba happily running along the beach!

'By some sort of miracle, she was alive,' said Tim. A vet's visit revealed only a bruised eye and a scratched tummy.

Curiosity nearly killed the cat when Sooty climbed into a washing machine motor. Owner Julie Gamman rushed into her kitchen when she heard anguished cries 50 minutes after putting on a wash. She could hear her kitten meowing frantically from inside the water and, when she turned the machine off and pulled it away from the wall, she could see a little head poking out from the motor.

'I felt sick,' said Julie. 'I was certain he'd die.'

Sooty had been investigating the loose backing plate when he got sucked in. The fire brigade managed to free the soggy moggie, who was taken to the vet still attached to part of the motor.

Alex Roebuck's two dogs had different walking habits. Sasha, the Siberian husky, roamed on a long lead while Tess, a greyhound–collie cross, loved to rush off chasing wildlife.

On a cold February day, when there had been 10 degrees of frost, Alex took the dogs for a walk along the local canal. As they headed home, Tess did a runner and Alex heard a crash. He ran to the canal but couldn't see Tess anywhere. Then he spotted the sheet of ice moving and realised she was trapped underneath in the icy water. As Alex contemplated having to plunge in to save his dog, Sasha launched herself into the canal, shattering the ice and freeing Tess. Using her powerful limbs as icebreakers, she swam towards Tess, grabbed her by the scruff of her neck and paddled back to the shore. Alex helped haul his pets out by pulling on the lead still attached to Sasha.

'I just couldn't believe what I was seeing,' said Alex. 'Tess would have died if Sasha hadn't saved her.'

Animal lover Winifred Skiff developed an affinity for Beauty the blind pony, one of dozens of animals she cared for at her Hampshire animal sanctuary. Winifred, too, was losing her sight and could understand the old pony's plight. It was an affinity that saved her life.

She was mucking out the horses on a wet, cold February afternoon when she slipped in the mud and fell backwards. Her sanctuary helpers had gone home and no one heard her cries for help in the high winds and lashing rain. She lay in excruciating pain, unable to move, while the mud crept into her clothing and weighed her down. The field was turning into a giant bog. Weeping with fear and frustration, Winifred thought she would die from hypothermia – until she saw a black shape looming through the darkness.

It was Beauty, whose sharp ears had picked up her mistress's cries. But Winifred feared the pony wouldn't see her and would trample on her. She called out 'whoa' and Beauty obeyed. Then the animal slowly inched her way backwards in the direction of Winifred's voice, until Winifred was able to stretch out her pain-wracked arthritic hands and hold on to the tail.

Instructing Beauty to 'walk on', Winifred was pulled from the mire to safety.

Miracles came three at a time in Pam Sica's life, thanks to her elderly dog. Her vet advised her to have 16-year-old Bullet put down when a massive tumour was found on his liver. She believes that, if she and husband, Troy, hadn't taken out a £2,500 loan to pay for

Bullet's treatment, their baby son wouldn't be alive today.

Against the odds, Bullet survived the surgery. Then, after years of trying, Pam became pregnant with her son, also named Troy. When the baby was 20 days old, Bullet began barking persistently. He kept racing between the kitchen and the hallway in Pam's home in Bellport, New York, and jumping up at his mistress.

Finally, Pam went to check on the baby and found him blue and lifeless in his cot. Paramedics told her that ten seconds longer and Troy might have died or suffered severe brain damage through lack of oxygen.

The golden retriever was given a Dog Hero of the Year Award for saving Troy.

Peppi the poodle made an amazing recovery after a tumour the size of a rugby ball was found in her stomach. It weighed a massive 4.5lb – a third of the pooch's entire body weight.

'It's hard to believe that something so big was inside a small dog like Peppi,' said owner

Catherine Moorcroft, of Willenhall, West Midlands. The tumour was the largest the vet had ever seen.

In an animal kingdom version of David and Goliath, a 7lb dachshund fought off a 1,000lb bear to save his master's life. Goeran Ryman was hunting in a Swedish forest when the bear struck. 'It came bounding towards me, a wall of brute force,' he recalled. 'I didn't even have time to raise my gun.

'I just thought to myself, "My God, what a way to die."'

The bear lashed out one giant paw and the lethal claws split open Goeran's head. As he lay unconscious with terrible wounds, brave Birk, the sausage dog, came bounding out of the forest, grabbed the beast by the genitals and wouldn't let go until it turned and fled. Goeran, who needed 165 stitches in his face and body, said there's no doubt that Birk saved his life.

They say only cats have nine lives but Beau, the boxer, would like to challenge that. In nine years, he went through a glass window – twice – when he was trying to get out of the house while his owners were away; has been hit by a truck; has had life-threatening kidney failure; has had cancer and bowel problems; has been suspended by his back leg upside down on a fence for several hours; has had two cancerous tumours removed, one from his eyelid; and, while at the vet clinic, he pulled out his IV, broke out of his cage and set off the alarm

'It's a miracle he's still alive,' said owner Mike Daugherty.

Kyle the cat used up most of his nine lives when he was trapped in the rafters of a Clackmannanshire garage roof for seven weeks without food or water.

Rescuers in Scotland believe the three-year-old stayed alive by licking condensation, which had formed on the roof tiles.

Great-grandmother Ruth Gay was walking her two-year-old dog, Blue, along the canal in Fort Meyers, Florida, when she slipped and broke both shoulders. While she lay in agony, unable to move, a six-foot alligator crawled out of the water and started moving towards her.

Although it could have swallowed 44lb Blue whole, the little dog charged the reptile in an attempt to frighten him away. Ruth, 86, heard Blue howl in pain. Then everything went quiet.

'I was sure he was dead,' she said.

When her family arrived home more than an hour later, they found Blue covered in blood from multiple puncture wounds. Despite his severe injuries, he kept barking until they followed him and he led them to Ruth.


It's not just dogs and cats whose miraculous behaviour saves lives. Lulu, the one-eyed pet kangaroo, is the heroine in the Richards family after she raised the alarm when her master was injured.

Australian farmer, Len, was checking for

storm damage on his farm in Victoria when a branch fell and hit him on the head, knocking him unconscious. Lulu hopped to the family's farmhouse and raised the alarm by repeatedly rapping on the back door and making barking noises. When the family went to investigate, Lulu led them to Len, where she stood upright with her chest puffed out protectively over his body.

The Richards said Lulu, who was adopted as a baby after her mother was killed, acted more like a pet dog than a wild kangaroo.

The Burk family pet was a piglet they'd hand-raised at their Texas home. One hot summer day, Carol and her 11-year-old mentally handicapped son, Anthony, went for a swim in the local lake with two-month-old Priscilla, the piglet. At the end of a happy but exhausting day, Carol got out of the water to dry herself. When she turned round, she saw Anthony far out in the deep water, desperately trying to keep afloat.

She jumped back into the lake and began swimming furiously towards him, but the 22lb piglet was already on the way. When Priscilla reached Anthony, he grabbed on to her halter and leash. But, in his panic, he pulled too hard and they both went under water. He was four times her weight and Priscilla struggled to get back to the surface. Eventually, she managed to start swimming again, with Anthony clinging to her small body.

For her heroism, she was honoured with a Priscilla the Pig day in Houston.

Eighty days after a devastating earthquake struck Taiwan, killing about 2,400 people in September 1999, a cat was discovered alive in the ruins of a collapsed building. Dehydrated and barely breathing, it had lost half its body weight, but, after treatment, made a full recovery.

It's the longest post-earthquake survival by a cat.

A wheelchair-bound diabetic owes his life many times over to the pet he rescued from a dog's home. Adrian Lynn's condition was so severe it meant he could slip into a coma without warning. He had passed out in the street on several occasions and it made him terrified to go out.

While he was at the Scottish Society for the Protection of Animals looking at potential pets, Pixie appeared and jumped straight on to his lap.

'Pixie chose me rather than me choosing her,' said Adrian.

The dog's extraordinary sense of smell tells her when Adrian's blood sugar level drops and she fusses until Adrian has something to eat to prevent hypoglycaemia.

'She has saved my life several times and saved me at least 12 trips to hospital,' said Adrian. 'She's my canine guardian angel.'

Pedro the Border collie was rescued from a Welsh dog's home by owner Maureen Porter. Ten years later, Pedro was able to return the favour when 69-year-old Maureen fell in her garden and broke her hip.

Her husband, Eric, was away and there were no neighbours to hear her cries for help from their country cottage near Cardigan. Pedro sensed her plight and spent the next 18 hours keeping his body close to hers to keep her warm. When Eric couldn't reach Maureen by phone the next morning, the village shop-keeper checked and found Maureen lying on the ground.

'Pedro saved her life,' said a grateful Eric. 'One rescue deserves another.'

Animals have been known to exhibit remarkable psychic powers that defy explanation. Biologist Dr Rupert Sheldrake conducted extensive studies in this field, especially into animals' ability to know when their owners were arriving home.

A terrier called Jaytee always sat in the window of his Lancashire home at the same time each day, waiting for his mistress, Pam, to come home. When she lost her job and started coming home at different times, the dog still went to the window and waited for her at the correct time.

Using a film crew who didn't know Pam's movements, Dr Sheldrake was able to prove that the dog somehow sensed when Pam was starting her journey home.

A pet's devotion knows no bounds:

• A Japanese dog, who used to meet his master at a Tokyo railway station after work, continued to do so every day for ten years after his master died of a heart attack.

• King, the German shepherd, ran away from his New York home on the day of his master's funeral. Three weeks later, the dead man's family discovered from the cemetery groundsman that the dog had been going to his master's grave every day and howling. No one can explain how he knew where it was.

• When Moggie's elderly owner died, the cat vanished. Two days later, friends attending the funeral 15 miles away in an Oxfordshire village saw Moggie sitting on a nearby gravestone. She had never been to the area before and couldn't have known where the funeral was going to be held.

The ship was being relentlessly pounded against the rocks and the 93 crew and passengers huddled in terror, fearing their end was imminent. Around them, stormy seas lashed the coast of Newfoundland, Canada, making it impossible to disembark. It was too far for ropes thrown by the crew to reach people watching on the shore, but one brave sailor took a rope and jumped into the seething ocean, attempting to swim to the beach. He was never seen again.

The captain of the Ethie realised their last hope lay in the ship's dog, Tang, a Newfoundland. He gave the rope to the dog and, with it clasped in his mouth, Tang jumped into the sea. Battling the huge waves and strong undertow, Tang made for land as onlookers urged him on. After nail-biting minutes, Tang flopped exhausted on to the sand and the rope was secured to enable the passengers to leave their sinking ship.

Lloyd's of London gave Tang a medal for his bravery.

New Zealand lifeguard Rob Howes was swimming in the sea with his daughter and two of her friends when a pod of dolphins started circling them. They swam in tight circles around the group, like a dog herding sheep. Whenever Rob tried to break away, two of the bigger dolphins pushed him back.

He couldn't understand what was going on, until he spotted a ten-foot great white shark cruising towards them. The man-eater was deterred by the ring of dolphins and swam away.

# CHAPTER SEVEN:
## Healing

# HEALING

Life took a horrifying wrong turn for 21-year-old Mitchell May when he was involved in a head-on collision on a rain-drenched road in Alabama, USA. He was flown to a California hospital in a full body cast, with a collapsed lung and a leg shattered in 40 places. Plastic surgeons declared his leg unsalvageable.

'From just below the knee down to the ankle, there was just bare bone,' remembers orthopaedic surgeon Edgar Dawson. 'The leg was grossly infected. It had to come off.'

Mitchell flatly refused. His mother Mary

sought out a healer, Jack Gray, who was noted for his eccentric appearance and unorthodox methods. Gray stayed by Mitchell's side 12 hours a day, employing a mixture of laying-on of hands, hypnosis and prayer.

Within three days, Mitchell's constant and agonising pain had gone. Over the next few months, the two-inch gap in Mitchell's bone began to regenerate, the missing nerve and muscle tissue filled in and the fractures began to fuse. Eventually, and against all medical prognoses, Mitchell regained full use of his leg. Asked to explain how this could have happened, Dr Dawson replied, 'It was a miracle.'

They called him The Miracle Worker. He could accomplish the seemingly impossible, opening up a new world for severely handicapped children and their families. Using a method of mental exercising he developed over 50 years, coupled with his indefatigable optimism, Professor Reuven Feuerstein has saved children from a life languishing in a mental hospital or institution.

Those labelled by experts as 'morons' or 'imbeciles' have been taught to read and write, to walk and talk.

Gemma Winton was battered by her nanny when she was six weeks old and suffered a severe brain haemorrhage. Doctors told her mother, Cheryl, that Gemma would never be anything more than a moron. Mrs Winton, unable to cope with Gemma's severe handicaps, eventually put her daughter into a residential home.

By the time she was ten, Gemma could barely talk, she was doubly incontinent and she dribbled constantly. Her grandfather took her to Professor Feuerstein, who spent four years working with her at his institute in Jerusalem. At the end of her stay, she was no longer incontinent, she had stopped dribbling and she spoke in proper sentences, in both English and Hebrew.

Another of the professor's patients was Flora Keays, daughter of Lord Parkinson, who developed a severe form of epilepsy as a child. Her mother, Sara, says Feuerstein 'worked some kind of miracle' with her child.

As the train snaked its way towards the healing springs at Lourdes in the spring of 1903, the doctor filled a syringe with morphine and administered it to his dying patient, assuring her the pain would soon be gone.

In his heart, he doubted that Marie Bailly would even survive the journey. Both her parents had died from the untreatable condition, which was destroying her young body. But she had begged to go to Lourdes, knowing it was her last hope. Dr Alexis Carrel viewed miraculous cures with scepticism, arguing that organic disease could not be reversed. Using Marie Bailly as an example, he announced to colleagues that, if she could be cured, it would indeed be a miracle.

When he returned to the hospital near Lourdes where Marie had been admitted after the journey, she was at death's door. Her heart was racing at 150 beats a minute and her entire body was swollen.

Marie's distraught companion urged Dr Carrel to take Marie to the pools at Lourdes, but

194

he feared she would die on the way. Accepting that she had nothing to lose, he agreed. His patient was too ill to be immersed into the pool, so the attendants instead sprinkled drops of water over her bloated abdomen.

As she rested later, Dr Carrel examined Marie and was astounded to see that her abdomen was no longer distended and her heartbeat had stabilised. Not long after, she began to speak and then sat up and moved around. A few days later, her body was totally and inexplicably cured.

Dr Carrel had witnessed his miracle. His testimony provided the medical world with evidence that miracles can be observed and studied by means of conventional science.


The healing of a child has special poignancy. Four-year-old Francis Pascal was left blind and totally paralysed by meningitis.

In August 1938 he was taken on a pilgrimage to Lourdes where his mother immersed him in the healing baths. He went into convulsions and shrieked like a wounded animal with the shock of the cold water.

Two days later, his mother hesitantly returned to the baths and this time Francis didn't cry out. He then asked his mother to take him to the Basilica and, as she pushed his wheelchair up the slope towards the church, Francis stretched out his arm and pointed to a man in an invalid carriage.

His sight had returned. Three months later, he felt sensation in his legs and, when his mother helped him to his feet, he could walk. Twelve doctors wrote confirming that the child had been completely cured at Lourdes, a cure which 'cannot be explained in terms of the ordinary laws of nature', according to one.

In the 157 years since the Virgin Mary was reported to have appeared to Bernadette Soubirous at Lourdes, tens of millions of cases have been put forward for miracle status. Only 66 of the 7,000 healings considered have been officially recognised as being miracles.

'There probably should have been more,' said Patrick Theillier, head of the Lourdes Medical Bureau, 'but many pilgrims don't even report the disappearance of their sickness.'

A healing must meet several strict medical criteria before it can be considered a miracle: the patient must be gravely ill, suffering from a known disease that was diagnosed by medical professionals; the illness must not be psychological; the condition must be impossible to cure through conventional treatment; the cure must be instant and complete; once a cure has been confirmed, the case goes to the Lourdes International Medical Committee, comprising physicians from 75 countries, which can take 10 to 15 years to decide if a cure defies medical explanation.

The most recently recognised Lourdes miracle healing involves a Frenchman who was paralysed by multiple sclerosis.

When he was 51, Jean-Pierre Bely went to Lourdes and was anointed. When he returned home, he was already able to walk and has since recovered completely. Patrick Fontanaud, an agnostic physician who looked after Bely, said there is no scientific explanation for what happened.

The *British Medical Journal* reported the case of a woman who went to her doctor because she was hearing voices telling her she was seriously ill and needed help.

Dr Ikechukwu Azuonye, believing his patient's problems were in her mind, prescribed medication and referred her for counselling, which helped. While she was on holiday with her husband, the voices returned, urging her to return to England for medical care. They even gave her an address to go to, which turned out to be a hospital specialising in brain tumours.

The woman returned to her doctor and insisted she had a brain scan, which he reluctantly agreed to despite opposition from his colleagues. The scan showed she was indeed suffering from a tumour, which was operated on successfully.

In a radio interview, Dr Azuonye said that if it hadn't been for the voices, the woman would have died.

There have been many documented cases of people claiming the bleeding wounds of Jesus Christ suddenly appeared on their own bodies.

As most of these stigmatics lived hundreds of years ago, it's impossible to examine their credibility. But it's more difficult to dismiss the relatively recent examples such as the Italian priest, Padre Pio, who awoke one morning in 1918 bleeding profusely from his hands, feet and side. These wounds, which extended completely through his hands, never healed throughout the following 50 years of his life, despite medical treatments. He also developed the powers of bilocation (the ability to be in two places at the same time), healing and prophecy.

Padre Pio, who died in 1968, was banished

by his church and made to live a virtual prisoner in his small village. Even so, he became one of the best-known and most sought-after miracle workers. When his canonisation was announced in 2002, hundreds of people came forward with testimonies of how the priest had helped them.

Richard Butler, an Irish pensioner, lost all his toes to diabetes. One day he had to walk a mile to a petrol station and his feet started bleeding heavily. Not even the best plastic surgeons could help Richard, whose feet continued to bleed for three months, robbing him of the ability to walk again. A friend visited him in hospital with a relic of the priest's and prayed for Richard's recovery. The next morning, he was perfectly healed and could walk home.

The most recent case of stigmata came from an American suburb, Lake Ridge, Virginia, in 1991 where Father James Bruse began bleeding from the wrists and feet. A year later, the Madonna statue in his church wept in front of 500 people.

In recent years, unearthly experiences have sometimes been attributed to the intervention of angels though, not surprisingly, many people are reluctant to admit to them. Those who do are often at great pains to emphasise that they couldn't have invented what they saw.

Ann Cannady can never forget the day she received the results of a third test confirming that she had advanced uterine cancer. Her husband, Gary, had lost his first wife to the same type of cancer and couldn't bear the thought of going through it again.

Three days before she was due in hospital for major surgery, the doorbell rang. Standing on the step was a tall black man with deep-blue eyes. He introduced himself as Thomas and told Ann her cancer had gone.

'How do you know my name and that I have cancer?' stammered Ann.

The man came into the house and held up his hand in front of Ann's body. She felt an incredible heat flowing from it and then she fainted. When she had recovered, Ann called the hospital and insisted that they perform another biopsy before starting the surgery. The doctor agreed reluctantly, on condition that, if it came back positive, they would proceed immediately.

When Ann woke up, the doctor was at her bedside. 'I don't understand it, but your test came back clean,' he said. Ann says he later acknowledged that he'd 'witnessed a miracle'.

Rodolfo Gonzalez was an up-and-coming boxer with a string of winning fights and a promising career ahead of him. Then the young Mexican was KO'd by an enemy he couldn't vanquish – cancer. He consulted several doctors in California who told him the inoperable disease was spreading from a large tumour on his liver to his stomach, kidneys, chest and heart.

In desperation, he went to see one last medic who, after an exhaustive round of tests, delivered the death sentence. At 27, Rodolfo had two months to live. He decided to return to Mexico to spend his final days with his mother in Tijuana. Lying in bed, he prayed for the end to come quickly to save his family from suffering. That night, he had a vision of the Virgin of Guadalupe who told him to come to her church.

The next day, Rodolfo shuffled painfully along to the cathedral where he knelt in the empty building and prayed.

'I began to feel a warm sensation coming from the Virgin and flowing through my body,' he said. 'My pain began to diminish and I could breathe easily.'

After four months, Rodolfo returned to Los Angeles where his manager said he would need medical clearance before he would be allowed to box again. He went back to his doctors who were astounded that his cancer had gone completely.

'They said it was a miracle that I was alive,' he said. 'They had no medical explanations for my cure.'

Rodolfo went on to become Lightweight Champion of the World.

Marguerite Otton was suffering from breast cancer. 'The doctors had given me three to six months,' she said. 'They told me further treatment would be useless.' In desperation, Marguerite, a former nurse from Margate, Kent, went to see healer Matthew Manning. Marguerite describes the experience: 'The heat from his hands was incredible. When he put them near me, I felt a shooting pain.

'On my skin afterwards, I found marks, as if a flat iron had been pressed against me.'

After a year of visits, Marguerite was cured. She is one of hundreds of people who have sought healing help from Manning. Among those who have consulted him are John Cleese, Van Morrison, Pope Paul VI and Maureen Lipman. Prince Philip even asked for his help with a wrist problem during a dinner at Buckingham Palace.

The thing that sets healer Matthew Manning apart from the others is that he has invited scientific scrutiny rather than avoiding it. In Texas, under the supervision of American scientist Dr John Kmetz, of the Science

Unlimited Research Foundation, he attempted to kill off cancer cells using mental energy. In 27 out of 30 trials, Dr Kmetz recorded a reduced cell count.

Manning has the support of many leading specialists, including Professor Karol Sikora, consultant oncologist at London's Hammersmith Hospital and former head of the World Health Organisation's cancer programme. Sikora says Manning has a 'remarkable track record' as a healer.

In 1868, a Belgian peasant called Pierre de Rudder fell from a tree and broke his leg so badly that bone fragments had to be taken from the wound. The leg was so damaged that it couldn't be set and there was a gap of over an inch separating the upper and lower parts of the bone at the site of the fracture. The lower portion of the leg dangled freely, held in place only by skin and muscle tissue.

Despite the excruciating pain and advice to have the leg amputated, de Rudder refused, and lived with the agony for eight years before deciding to make a pilgrimage to Our Lady of Lourdes statue near Ghent.

Before de Rudder left, his leg was examined by Dr van Hoestenberghe who noted that the open wound was still unhealed and there was still a gap in the broken bone. The lower portion of the leg could be moved in all directions and could even be folded upwards.

The train journey was a nightmare for de Rudder and he was in a terrible state when he reached the town of Oostacker. Here he began to pray earnestly before the statue, asking for his sins to be forgiven and for his children to be cared for if he died. As he prayed, he felt something happening to him. Suddenly, he stood up without the aid of his crutches and began to walk.

Even more amazing was that not only had his leg been healed; the gap in the broken bone had also disappeared. Dr van Hoestenberghe couldn't believe it. After de Rudder's death, he was given permission to exhume the body and study the legs. Photographs he took clearly show that the two parts of the bone had been fused together by a new piece of healthy bone over an inch long. Such growth or regeneration of bone is medically unprecedented.

Today, de Rudder's leg bones are preserved at the University of Louvain in Belgium.

William Kent's faith gave him strength to cope after a devastating motorcycle accident left him a quadriplegic.

Despite massive brain and spinal injuries, the young American continued his education and excelled in wheelchair sports at national and international levels. But there were rough patches when he attempted suicide twice after losing the love of his life and his business.

In 2000, he returned to the church and felt drawn to attend a 5 November service at the World Harvest Church in Columbus, Ohio, 400 miles from his home. During the service, Pastor Rod Parsley called all those with certain illnesses to come forward. William joined them and, as he sat there, he felt something happening to his body. He went to adjust himself in the wheelchair and suddenly found he could stand – for the first time in over 15 years.

He was even able to walk up the steps towards the pulpit. After the service William, a diabetic, discovered that his blood sugar level had dropped from 470 to 128.

The miraculous healing of a dying multiple sclerosis victim dumbfounded the medical world and church authorities.

Marion Carroll was completely dependent on her husband, Jimmy, and their two children, who had to feed and change her. She was almost blind and her speech slurred. Her food had to be liquidised because she couldn't swallow solids and she also suffered from epilepsy, thyroid problems and a kidney infection. She had lost all power in her legs and her right arm, had no control over her bowel and bladder, and wore a neck brace because she could no longer support her head.

Marion was ready to die but only wanted to see her children grow out of their teens before she did so. One day, a friendly ambulance man asked her if she'd like to go to Knock Shrine in County Mayo, Ireland. Marion wasn't keen because she was due to have major kidney surgery the next day. Also, she'd been to the shrine before and found it 'a miserable place'.

But she was persuaded to go and, in the basilica, she was strapped on a stretcher under a statue of Our Lady of Knock. Marion prayed for her husband and children, that they would cope when she was gone. As she was anointed and took communion, she felt an unusual pain in her heels. Then the pain disappeared – along with every pain in her body.

When the priest began to bless the sick, Marion sensed a voice telling her to get up and walk. Afraid others would think she'd lost her mind, she waited until she was back in the St John's Ambulance area before she asked a friend to undo her stretcher straps.

'My legs swung out and I got up,' she recalled. 'I wasn't even stiff. My muscles were working even after three years in a wheelchair. And my speech was perfect.'

When she got home and walked in front of Jimmy, he got down on his knees and cried his heart out.

Marion was left with the power of healing and went on to help other sick people.

Mother Teresa was known the world over for her charitable works among the poor and sick, and won the 1979 Nobel Prize for Peace. In the process of declaring her a saint, the Vatican officially recognised as a miracle the healing of a Bengali tribal woman, Monika Besra, who was suffering from an abdominal tumour.

Besra, who was 30 at the time, said that on the day of the miracle she had seen light coming from a photo of Mother Teresa, who had died a year earlier. After an image of the nun was placed on her stomach, her tumour disappeared. This was judged by a panel of doctors to be without any medical explanation.

210

After three-year-old Audrey Santo fell into the family swimming pool and nearly drowned, she lapsed into a coma from which she never recovered.

Doctors recommended that her mother, Linda, put her into an institution to live out what little time she had left. But Linda refused and took Audrey, the youngest of her four children, home to the bedroom she had turned into an intensive care unit.

Against all advice, Linda then took Audrey on a pilgrimage from Massachusetts, USA, to Medjugorje, the remote site in former Yugoslavia where miracles are said to take place.

Linda was so confident that her child would be cured she brought her a pair of sandals for her to wear home. But, instead of a miracle, Audrey stopped breathing briefly and had to be flown home on an emergency medical plane.

Linda's mother mortgaged her house to pay Audrey's massive medical bill. Then Linda, whose husband, Steve, had left her, was diagnosed with breast cancer and went through a gruelling course of chemotherapy. It seemed as though the family could suffer no more.

One day in 1993, Linda was shocked to see that oil was pouring down a portrait of the Lady of Guadalupe hanging in her home. It was painted on canvas, without a glass covering, so there was no place for an oil source to be concealed. Within months oil was flowing from dozens of icons, statues, chalices and walls around the house. So copious were the quantities, Linda had to attach cups to collect it.

The Catholic Church set up a commission to investigate the weeping icons and, although no one has seen an object actually start to emit oil, the commissioners were astounded when a religious icon they had brought along oozed oil that night. The phenomenon quickly attracted pilgrims and priests from all over the world who believed that Audrey possessed special powers. An annual Mass in Worcester, Massachusetts, to mark the anniversary of the day Audrey nearly drowned draws thousands of believers. Many more have made a pilgrimage to Audrey's bedside where miraculous healings have been attributed to her.

Joey Parolisi, 18, believes Audrey Santo is

responsible for saving his life after a serious motorcycle accident. Doctors said he'd be lucky to live but, if he did, he would certainly never walk again. Joey was airlifted to Boston where he spent five months in hospital. During this time his mother, Sheryle, started praying through Audrey. Soon after Joey was taken to see Audrey, his condition started to improve and, one day, he stood up and walked without his cane or crutches.

Leo Perras had been in a wheelchair for 21 years, paralysed after an operation to rectify a back injury.

As his leg muscles atrophied through lack of use, arthritis set in, which caused him great pain. He relied on regular doses of strong painkillers but life was miserable. Then his doctor advised him to attend a healing service conducted by Father DiOrio, a priest and school psychologist.

Within minutes of the priest praying over him, Leo stood up and walked away from his wheelchair, free of any pain. His family doctor, Mitchell Tenerowicz, chief of staff at Cooley Dickinson Hospital, Northampton, Massachusetts, was amazed at his patient's recovery. He examined Leo's legs, which were still atrophied, and said there was no way he was physically capable of walking. Yet the indisputable evidence was in front of him.

Glasgow dockworker John Fagan faced the inevitable prospect of death as his body succumbed to cancer.

His wife refused to admit him to a hospice and cared for him at home. One of the few visitors who came in the last lonely stages of his life was Father John Fitzgibbon, who delivered the last rites one bleak January day. Before he left, the priest gave John's wife a medal of Blessed John Ogilvie and told her to pray to the martyr, a Scottish holy man who was executed in 1614.

John's condition continued to deteriorate and he vomited continually. Then, in March, a prayer group gathered round his bed.

When John's physician, Dr Archibald MacDonald, arrived later, he told Mrs Fagan he would return the next day to sign the death certificate as his patient couldn't possibly survive much longer. But when Mrs Fagan went into her husband's room the next morning expecting to find a corpse, John sat up and told her he was hungry. She rushed to call the doctor, who was equally amazed by the change in John. His pain had gone, the vomiting had stopped and he went on to make a complete recovery.

The case became one of the most thoroughly documented healings reported in modern time and was declared a miracle after a panel of eminent doctors, at the end of two years, could find no medical explanation for the cure.

Terminal cancer patient Mrs Patricia Bitzan, from St Cloud, Minnesota, was given three months to live. She made a pilgrimage to Belgium and prayed at the tomb of Dublin-born monk Dom Columba Marmion.

On her return to America, doctors found her

cancer had disappeared. It was this miracle that passed the scrupulous examination by a specialised medical team in Rome and led to the monk's journey to sainthood.

During the process of studying Marmion's life to determine whether or not he qualified, his body was exhumed. When the carpenters opened the coffin, witnesses were astounded to see that, even after 40 years in the grave, there was no decay on the body. After years of researching the case, theologians, historians and doctors concluded that the disappearance of Mrs Bitzan's cancer had no scientific explanation and defied all the odds against her survival.

In December 1999, Pope John Paul II publicly acknowledged the event as a miracle.

Indian guru Sai Baba is regarded by his followers around the world as a divinity in human form. Thousands of miracles have been attributed to him, from manifesting jewellery to turning water into petrol. He heals the sick with the aid of vibhuti, or sacred wood ash, which apparently appears from nowhere as he waves his hand.

The most astonishing display of his power reportedly took place in 1953 when he brought back to life a blue and stiff body. In 1971, he is also supposed to have revived Walter Cowan, a man declared dead from a heart attack.

Among others who claim Sai has healed them is Irish cancer sufferer Iris Riddell. After drastic surgery, followed by intense chemotherapy, she prayed to Sai Baba and, despite a grim prognosis, was given the all-clear by her doctors within 14 months of her initial diagnosis. Iris, who has visited the guru's ashram in Indian three times, said, 'When you are in the presence of Sai Baba, you feel something very special.'

For 27 years, Jean Neil was confined to a wheelchair, paralysed by a fall and in constant excruciating pain from this and other ailments. Only her loving family saved her from suicide as she endured 15 operations on her spine, then the crushing blow of a car accident, which left her almost blind.

One night, the grandmother from Rugby dreamed of being healed by a 'tall man with a foreign accent'. Six weeks later, Jean, 57, attended a Pentecostal youth rally in Birmingham led by German Pastor Reinhard Bonnke, and she immediately recognised him as being the man in her dreams. In the middle of the service, Pastor Bonnke caught sight of Jean and pushed his way through the crowd to reach her.

'He put his hands on my shoulders and suddenly a surge of warmth and energy flooded through my body,' recalled Jean. 'A pain like a hot knife shot into my spine.'

When the pastor told her to get up and walk, she stood up from her wheelchair and ran towards the stage with tears running down her face as 12,000 spectators cheered.

Her doctor confirmed that Jean had, inexplicably, been totally cured of all her illnesses. She went on to swim, jog, horse ride and hang-glide.

218

# CHAPTER EIGHT

# Endurance and Feats

# ENDURANCE AND FEATS

For a small group of people, 'living on thin air' is more than an expression. It's a way of life. Known as Breatharians, they believe – and back their belief with their existence – that the body can survive without food.

Barbara Moore, MD, gradually reduced her intake of nutrients over 20 years until she consumed only water flavoured with a few drops of lemon juice. When interviewed by the London Sunday Chronicle in 1951, the reporter said she looked closer to 30 than 50.

'There is so much more in sunlight and air

than can be seen by the naked eye or with scientific instruments,' she explained.

Every year she went to Switzerland to climb mountains, drinking only water from the streams for three months. When she wasn't climbing, she walked 30 to 40 miles a day. Her body became impervious to heat and cold, hunger or fatigue, and she needed only three hours' sleep a night.

'As my body is free of toxins, I'm never ill,' she said. 'I hope in time to live entirely on air.'

Ironically, Barbara Moore was hit by a car and killed while walking across America.

Autotrophs, another name for non-eaters, can fast for years. Indian yogi Pralad Djani stopped eating at six years old. When he was 70, doctors examined and observed him for ten days using surveillance cameras and a sealed bathroom. Although he ate and drank nothing, they found that his body and mind were functioning absolutely normally.

Russia's most famous autotroph, Zinaida Baranova, had been living without food or water for four and a half years when scientists at the Bauman Institute investigated and reported that the 67-year-old woman's biological age corresponded to a 20-year-old's. She was perfectly healthy and all her organs were in good condition. The experts said she was very energetic and free from any diseases.

A Frenchwoman is also reported to have survived for more than two decades without eating or drinking. Known as Madame R, she maintained perfect health by consuming only Communion wafers since she had begun a total fast. Not only did she not lose weight, her doctors said she actually gained 59lb.

In an experiment in 1980, the doctors locked Madame R in a convent cell for 47 days without food or water.

'According to medical science, no human being can survive such a long period without food or liquid,' said Dr Phillipe Lorron of the Salpetrierre Hospital in Paris. 'But Madame R made it and was in good health at the end of the experiment. I can't give any scientific explanation for the phenomenon.'

When seven-year-old Jean-Luc Archer ran into the path of a BMW near his Manchester home, there was little hope of saving him. He was trapped beneath the wheels of the one-and-a-half-ton car, which was crushing him to death.

Lisa Hodgkinson arrived on the scene and instinctively started trying to lift the car off the boy's body. At first, she couldn't budge it. Then she tried to heave it forward and somehow summoned the superhuman strength to slowly inch it off Jean-Luc.

'I can't explain how I did it,' said 30-year-old Lisa. 'I must have thought I was the Incredible Hulk.'

She gave the boy mouth-to-mouth resuscitation until an ambulance arrived but he was so badly injured the doctors gave him only a 30 per cent chance of survival.

Jean-Luc fought back with such determination that he went home three weeks later, where he was welcomed by the rescuer he calls Wonderwoman.

An Icelandic fishing captain known as The Iceman grabbed a 660lb shark with his bare hands, hauled it from the water and killed it.

Captain Sigurdur Petursson, skipper of the trawler Erik the Red, was on a beach in Kuummiit, east Greenland, watching his crew processing a catch when he saw the shark swimming towards them, lured by the fish blood and innards. He ran into the shallow water and seized the shark by its tail. Then he dragged it off to dry land and slaughtered it with his knife.

Captain Petursson earned his nickname because of his fearless character.

The weird phenomenon of spontaneous human combustion continues to baffle experts. What makes a person's body suddenly ignite? How can it reach the incredible temperatures necessary to cremate flesh and bones?

• Early one morning in 1967 passers-by on a London street noticed a light from inside a derelict house and called the fire brigade. When the crew broke into the building they couldn't believe their eyes. Lying at the bottom of the stairs was a man with a blue flame, as bright as a blowtorch, shooting from a slit in his stomach. Nothing else in the house was on fire – just the body of local alcoholic Robert Bailey, who seemed to be burning from inside. Even his clothing was undamaged, except for the area around his abdomen.

The gas and electricity supplies had been disconnected and no matches were found. Firefighters extinguished the flame with some difficulty and the death was filed under 'unknown causes'.

• A 61-year-old mentally handicapped woman burst into flames in front of her father as they sat in the kitchen of their home in Edmonton, London, in 1982. He saw a flash of light and looked up to see his daughter, Jeannie Saffin, with flames roaring from her face and stomach like a dragon. Again, the room was undamaged by the fire, which was confined only to the victim's body.

• When 67-year-old Mrs Mary Reeser was found in her Florida flat, the 12-stone woman had been reduced to a 10lb pile of charred remains. Experts said that a temperature of 2,500 degrees Fahrenheit is necessary for such a thorough cremation – a cigarette igniting her clothing could not have achieved that.

In one of the most extraordinary feats of human endurance seen in Britain, 19th-century athlete Robert Barclay bet 1,000 guineas that he could walk 1,000 miles in 1,000 hours – and won. Each mile had to be walked in a separate hour, day and night, and he spent 41 days without sleeping for more than 90 minutes at a time.

Barclay, 30, was a Scottish aristocrat and landowner who enjoyed the fashionable sport of pedestrianism – walking to win a wager. In 1809, he accepted the bet, which would net twice the average farm labourer's annual wage, although most people believed he would fail.

Gas lamps were set on poles at 100-yard intervals along the course around Newmarket, and he carried a pair of pistols to ensure his safety. In the third week of the race, he suffered from strained ligaments in his right knee, and in the fourth he developed toothache.

One morning, when his manservant took him to the starting line to begin the 607th mile, Barclay – although standing up – was in fact asleep. His servant had to beat him violently with a walking stick to wake him.

Barclay completed the last mile 23 minutes inside the deadline, to national acclaim and great wealth. After his first continuous sleep for nearly 42 days, he was weighed on the Newmarket scales and had lost 32lb during his epic walk.

Lisa Fittipaldi thought her life was over when an eye condition slowly robbed her of her sight. All she wanted to do was stay in her room and grieve.

Then a friend persuaded her to go on a two-week painting course in Louisiana. Despite her handicap, Lisa enjoyed the session so much she was inspired to learn all she could about painting.

'I taught myself how to feel if a paint pigment and watercolour was yellow, blue or red,' she said. She perfected a technique called 'mental mapping', which helped her find where she was on the canvas, and soon she was creating beautiful life scenes in intricate detail.

Lisa went on to exhibit at major galleries and to sell her work widely. No one quite understands how she accomplishes her art without sight.

American Angelo Faticoni was dubbed The Human Cork because he could stay afloat in water for 15 hours with 20lb of lead tied to his ankles.

He could sleep in water, roll up into a ball, lie on his side or assume any other position asked of him. Once he was sewn into a bag and thrown headfirst into the water with a 20lb cannonball tied to his legs. His head reappeared on the surface soon afterwards and remained motionless for eight hours.

Faticoni died in Florida in 1931 without ever revealing the secret of his miraculous feats.

Most people wouldn't go near a scorpion, but Kanchana Ketkeaw spent 32 days in a glass box with 3,400 poisonous stingers!

The 30-year-old Thai set an unofficial world record for the feat, during which she was stung nine times. She says she has built up immunity to their venom. The extraordinary endurance test was held in a 130-square-foot room in a Pattaya department store near Bangkok. Her only problem: insomnia, because the store closed later than Kanchana's usual bedtime.

Doug Goodale cut off his own arm to save his life after an accident at sea.

The lobster fisherman from Maine, USA, had become caught in a winch hauling lobster pots up from the seabed. The winch pulled him up so that he was hanging over the side of the boat, unable to either free himself or clamber back on board. He was alone and helpless in a boat being buffeted by stormy weather.

'Nobody near me. No help. No radio. That's it. I'm going to die,' he thought. Somehow he managed to struggle on to the deck, dislocating his shoulder in the process. But his arm was still trapped in the winch and bleeding badly. His only option was to pick up a knife and cut through his right arm.

Thinking of how much he wanted to live for his daughters, he did the unthinkable and severed his limb. Then he managed to pilot his boat back into harbour to get medical help.

'When I hear my six-year-old tell me it doesn't matter that I've only got one arm, I know I did the right thing,' he said.

Daniel Tammet, 26, doesn't need an address book. He has memorised every name and number he needs, which is nothing to a man who can learn a new language in 15 hours or memorise 1,000 numbers in minutes, then recite them backwards.

His miraculous skills enable him to make any complex mathematical calculations presented to him, including reciting the numerical value of pi to 22,514 decimal places. Daniel attributes his incredible gift to a series of fits he suffered between the ages of three and six, which left him with computer-like mental powers. He started seeing numbers as patterns, shapes, textures or moving lights. He sees patterns and colours for words, too, which he can recall instantly.

Daniel, of Herne Bay, Kent, England, learned enough Icelandic in 15 hours to conduct a television interview in the language. He also taught himself Finnish, Spanish, Lithuanian, Esperanto, Romanian, Russian and Arabic.

When the driver in front of him on the M6 crashed into the central reservation and careered up an embankment, lorry driver Jim Walker leaped into action.

Using strength he didn't know he had, the 57-year-old pushed the car away from the trees it was wedged between, then turned the vehicle over on to its wheels. Driver Lorraine Barker was still trapped, pinned by the gear stick, so Jim bent it straight and dragged her clear before the car burst into flames.

'I don't know how I managed to do it,' said Jim.

Michel Lotito polished off a most unusual meal at Christmas in 1996. He ate the last parts of a Cessna light aircraft he'd been munching his way through for several years.

Michel, of Grenoble, France, had previously eaten 18 bicycles, 15 supermarket trolleys, seven television sets, six chandeliers, two beds, a computer and a pair of skis.

Falling and breaking a bone in your leg is painful enough. Imagine the bones of the lower leg being pushed through the knee joint on impact. Now imagine having to descend 20,000 feet down a mountain with this horrific injury.

That's what climber Joe Simpson had to do when he was stranded on a Peruvian mountain after his climbing partner had cut the rope that linked them in order to save his life.

Simon Yates and Joe were descending Siula

Grande in blizzard conditions, with a wind-chill factor of minus 80 degrees Fahrenheit, when Joe fell. Simon tried to lower his injured friend down in stages, which was working until Joe hit a patch of ice, slid over a cliff and was left suspended over a crevasse. Simon made the difficult decision to sever the rope rather than be pulled over the cliff too, and he returned to base camp assuming Joe had fallen to his death.

In a miraculous feat of courage and endurance, Joe spent four agonising days struggling back to the camp in sub-zero temperatures without food or water. As he couldn't scale the walls of the crevasse, he risked lowering himself deeper inside it, hoping to find a way out.

He found an opening, then he crawled down the mountain, suffering excruciating pain as he hauled his broken leg over the ice and hopped over rocks, following Simon's footprints back to the camp. By then, he had lost a third of his body weight and was near death.

'I felt very alone and very scared in that crevasse,' he recalled. 'My abiding memory is of

234

an appalling sense of loneliness and that's what stopped me from giving up. I wanted to be with somebody when I died.'

A 73-year-old Kenyan grandfather was tending his potato and bean crops when a leopard charged out of the long grass and leapt on him.

In an amazing feat, peasant farmer Daniel M'Mburugu dropped his machete, reached into the animal's mouth and tore out its tongue. The leopard let out a blood-curdling cry and loped off to die.

Asked what had made him rip out the leopard's tongue, the farmer explained that he had heard a voice telling him to drop his panga and thrust his hand into the animal's mouth, so he obeyed.

# CHAPTER NINE:
# Unexplained Phenomena

# UNEXPLAINED PHENOMENA

If a scrap of paper on the ground had blown away moments before Niven Mitchell walked by, he wouldn't be a millionaire today.

The former security officer was walking out of Leytonstone tube station in East London on his way home from work when he saw the small piece of white paper fluttering on the pavement. Something made him bend down and pick it up. A telephone number was written on it in blue biro.

Stopping by the newsagent to get a paper, Niven remembered he hadn't bought his lottery tickets. On a whim, he took the piece of paper out of his pocket and used a combination of the numbers to complete five lines on the lottery form.

On Saturday evening, he couldn't believe his eyes when he discovered he had five correct numbers in each of the first four lines on his form. Hardly daring to look again, he checked the last line – and found he'd got all six numbers and hit the jackpot!

'I was astonishingly calm,' he recalled. 'I lit a cigarette, changed channels to check the football scores and then shouted to my wife, Margaret, that we'd cracked it.'

Niven scooped £1.25 million and promptly gave up work.

It's one of the most enduring and controversial religious riddles of our age. For 800 years, experts have puzzled and argued over a piece of material some claim was used to wrap the body of Jesus after the crucifixion.

The Shroud of Turin shows a ghostly image of a man wearing a crown of thorns and bearing wounds on his front, back and right-hand side. It was first displayed in a French church in 1357 and eventually moved to Turin 200 years later. But it wasn't until 1978 that scientists were allowed to examine the shroud for the first time, although, after 120 hours scrutinising the cloth in minute detail, they couldn't come up with any answers.

A second study in 1988 allowed scientists to attempt carbon dating a sliver of the shroud. The negative results have since been dismissed when it was discovered the sample they were given was flawed.

The mystery that lingers over this miraculous relic may never be solved.

Hilary Russell's parents watched in horror as their six-year-old daughter was swept out to sea in a riptide. They stood momentarily paralysed with shock and fear. Before her father, Richard, could go in after the girl, they noticed a dark-haired man standing near Hilary.

'He just plucked her out of the water and held her in his arms,' said Richard.

Hilary's mother, Susan, was astonished by the effortless way the man strode back through the waves. As he reached the shore in Miami Beach, Florida, he placed the child in her mother's arms and the family embraced in tearful relief. But, when they turned to thank the man, he'd gone.

An Essex housewife was amazed when she looked at two of the apples her husband had bought from a Southend supermarket the previous day.

Though he had checked them carefully for bruises, deep indentations in the sign of a Christian cross had appeared on each of them overnight.

A young man who had recently passed his driving test set off to a friend's 18th birthday party. His mother was concerned because the journey involved a drive across the north of England's unpredictable Pennines in the depths of winter.

The first flurries of snow began to fall as Toby left for the drive home after the party. He had never driven in snow before and the blizzard was worsening by the minute. The car's windscreen wipers couldn't cope with the huge, swirling flakes, making visibility poor. Toby was exhausted and frightened, wondering if he would make it home safely. Just then, he spotted a welcome sight: the familiar and distinctive blue and white company van belonging to one of his parents' neighbours. The driver flashed his lights as he passed, then slowed down so Toby could follow him.

When they reached the street where they lived, the neighbour flashed his lights and waved goodbye, as a relieved Toby turned into his drive. The next morning, he told his parents about the kind neighbour. They exchanged nervous glances.

'Are you sure it was him?' asked his mother. Toby was sure, as he'd seen the man's name on the side of the vehicle. Toby's mother went out to check the neighbour's drive. The van was covered in snow and, according to the man's wife, it hadn't been moved since her husband's fatal heart attack three days earlier.

One of the most remarkable examples of divine signs appeared on Thursday, 21 September 1995, when Hindus all over the world witnessed the milk miracle. Milk is the sacred fluid of Hindus, regarded in much the same way as Holy Water in Christianity.

An Indian temple priest in the Punjab was told by a woman that her sister had dreamed one of their gods, Ganesh, would come to Earth to drink milk at 4am. Reluctantly he opened the temple and, as predicted, the statue of Ganesh accepted milk from a spoon.

The news spread like wildfire throughout India and beyond, and within hours millions of Hindus from Bangkok to Britain reported the same phenomenon happening.

By Friday afternoon it had stopped. No one could explain it, especially people like the English vicar whose milk was accepted from his spoon by the statue, nor the non-Hindu woman in Cheshire who reported that her four-foot statue of the Virgin Mary had accepted nine spoonfuls of milk.

A 12-year-old Lebanese girl shocked her family when she began weeping crystal tears.

Hasnah Mohamed Meselmani produced razor-sharp glass shards up to seven times a day during 1996, without any apparent injury to her eyes. Her father took her to a local ophthalmologist, Dr Araji, who studied the phenomenon for two weeks before declaring that the girl was weeping pieces of real crystal, but he had no explanation for it.

During an examination by another ophthalmologist at the American University Hospital in Beirut, more crystals oozed out of Hasnah's eyes. Experts took samples of the substance to their laboratories for analysis and confirmed that it was crystal.

Naturally, the family was accused of fraud but they maintain Hasnah couldn't possibly have faked the phenomenon in full view of television cameras when close-up shots showed the glass emerging from her retina. They also questioned how she could have performed the 'trick' without sustaining any injury to her eyes from glass shown to be sharp enough to cut paper.

It was an ordinary day. Coventry housewife Mandy Spraggett had just finished her housework and decided to put her feet up for a bit of a rest.

Suddenly she felt a strong urge to call her father. This was unusual, as, although they were close, she never called him during the day. He was the sort of dad you only called when you had something to say – idle chit-chat wasn't his thing.

So Mandy picked up the phone and made the call. If he didn't answer after three or four rings, she decided, she'd hang up as she always did, assuming he'd gone out. But after ten rings Mandy still couldn't put down the receiver. Then the ringing stopped as though someone had picked up, but no one spoke.

Mandy could hear bumping noises and what sounded like someone choking. Eventually her father's shocked voice told her he'd fallen asleep with a pan of chips on the hob. The fat had burst into flames and was seconds away from turning the house into an inferno. The toxic fumes had overcome her father until Mandy's phone call had woken him – a call she'll never know why she made.

'Something kept telling me not to put the phone down,' she said. 'It gives me the shivers to think about what might have happened if I'd called ten minutes later.'

A mass-produced statue of the Virgin Mary sitting in the living room of a retired Irish postmistress attracted pilgrims from around the world after it began weeping and moving.

Mary had owned the statue for a few years until, one day, her daughter told her to come quickly to see what was happening. Red liquid was trickling from one of the eyes and clear liquid from the other. The eyes were opening

247

and closing and then the figure actually turned in the box while Mary and her daughter watched with awe.

As word spread, 500 people a day flocked to the house to see the weeping statue. Mary claims that some of them have been healed from deadly illnesses after touching the statue's robe.

When events coincide too many times to be the result of chance, there is no rational explanation.

Albert Rivers and Betty Cheetham from Swindon in Wiltshire, England, shared a table with another couple for dinner at a Tunisian hotel. The other couple introduced themselves as Albert Cheetham and Betty Rivers. As they chatted, they also discovered: both couples were married on the same day and at the same time; both couples have two sons, born in the same years; both couples have five grand-children and four great-grandchildren; both wives had worked in post offices in their home towns; both husbands had worked in railway

248

workshops building carriages; both wives had lost their engagement rings; the wives had identical watch bracelets on which the same links had been repaired.

One of the most compelling modern miracles, according to researchers, happened in former Yugoslavia when two teenagers went for a walk in the countryside near the village of Medjugorje.

They saw what they thought was an apparition of the Virgin Mary, a young woman in a silver-grey dress and a white veil, carrying a baby in her arms. Two other girls arrived and also saw the vision. One was so scared she ran back to the village, sobbing. She persuaded two local boys to return and look and they, too, were astounded by what they saw.

The fact that makes this sighting so unusual is that it reappeared night after night in several places. During the next ten years, the six young people saw the vision an incredible total of 3,000 times, far more than any similar sighting. Many experts interviewed the children to see if they had made up their story. Dr Ludvik Stopar, a professor of psychiatry at the University of Maribor and a member of the International Commission of Doctors, conducted a battery of tests, but found the children perfectly normal.

In a drastic move to prove they were faking it, a theologian waited until one of the children was in a trance-like state, then jabbed her with a large needle, hoping to reveal her pretence. The girl fell forward but showed no reaction to the pain, despite blood soaking her blouse. The priest then jabbed her a second time, but still could provoke no response.

Mary Buckingham was a strong swimmer but one day, while on holiday in Gibraltar, she realised she'd gone out further than she had intended.

The beach was on the distant horizon and the sea was getting choppy as the sun sank. She set off swimming back to shore, but the swell was exhausting her. Panic mounted, and she began to resign herself to inevitable death.

Suddenly, the face of an elderly man appeared in front of her. He smiled, placed a firm hand beneath her chin and swam strongly in the traditional rescue stroke. As she sat recovering on the sand, Mary felt firm but gentle hands on her shoulders. Then she turned to thank her rescuer, only to find she was completely alone on the beach.

In July 1998 a three-mile-long drawing of an Aboriginal man appeared in the South Australian desert, 400 miles north of Adelaide.

The amazing, perfectly proportioned figure, which can be discerned only from 3,000 feet above it, was drawn on the earth with a 20-foot-wide gouged line. Its circumference measures ten miles.

No one knows how the mystery figure got there.

A penniless American mum and her two young sons faced a grim Thanksgiving celebration in their tiny one-bedroom flat. The only food they had was three hot dogs that Ivy Olson cooked for her boys. It broke her heart when they told her they were hungry as they walked back from an outing to the park.

As they climbed the stairs to their flat, an old lady came out of her door and said she had cooked Thanksgiving dinner for them and insisted they went in and joined her. Ivy was impressed that the woman seemed to know what food she liked and even where she worked. They left carrying boxes full of leftovers, enough to feed them for a week, and a feeling of warmth and gratitude.

The next day, Ivy washed the boxes she'd borrowed and went downstairs to return them to her new friend. But no one answered the door and when she peered in through the windows, the place was totally empty.

Shocked and confused, Ivy contacted the manager of the building and asked where the old lady had gone.

'That flat's been vacant for weeks,' he told a stunned Ivy.

Adam Riklis was saddened but not surprised when his 19-year-old son, Joey, announced he was dropping out of college and heading off to India to 'find himself'. The father assumed the normal teenage rebellion would pass. But when Joey also turned his back on his Jewish faith, Adam, a Holocaust survivor, threw his son out of their house in Cleveland, Ohio, and disowned him.

Six years later, Joey bumped into an old school friend in Bombay who told him that Joey's father had died from a heart attack. Joey was stricken with grief and guilt, sure he had killed his father by breaking his heart. He set off on a pilgrimage to Israel and headed for the Wailing Wall to pray for his father's forgiveness.

Following the example of others there, Joey wrote a prayer on a scrap of paper to push into a crevice of the wall in the belief that the stones were so holy requests were more likely to be granted.

But all the crevices were already crammed with notes and it took Joey nearly an hour to find what he thought was an empty crack. Sliding his paper into the space he dislodged another note, which fluttered to the ground. Curious, Joey unravelled the sheet and read, 'My dear son, Joey, if you should ever happen to come to Israel and somehow miraculously find this note, I want you to know that I always loved you.' The note was signed by Joey's father.

An image of the Virgin Mary, which appeared on one poor Mexican peasant's cloak, has not faded or rotted after more than 470 years.

Nor have scientists been able to detect how the most famous of all 'divine image' miracles was imprinted on the cloth. All experts from around the world can say is that the full colour portrait was applied to the coarse canvas cloth without a brush. Even later additions to the picture have faded while the original remains unaffected by time, wear or the environment.

The amazing cloak was worn by Juan Diego when he had a vision of the Virgin Mary in 1531. When, on her instructions, he went to tell the bishop that she wished a church to be

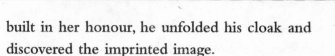

built in her honour, he unfolded his cloak and discovered the imprinted image.

The cloak is still on display at the Basilica of Our Lady of Guadalupe near Mexico City, as lifelike as it was on that day.